Catholic Church

A vindication of the Bull 'Apostolicae curae

Third Edition

Catholic Church

A vindication of the Bull 'Apostolicae curae
Third Edition

ISBN/EAN: 9783337109943

Printed in Europe, USA, Canada, Australia, Japan

Cover: Foto ©Lupo / pixelio.de

More available books at **www.hansebooks.com**

A VINDICATION

OF

THE BULL 'APOSTOLICÆ CURÆ'

A LETTER ON ANGLICAN ORDERS

BY THE
CARDINAL ARCHBISHOP AND BISHOPS OF
THE PROVINCE OF WESTMINSTER

IN REPLY
TO THE LETTER ADDRESSED TO THEM
BY THE
ANGLICAN ARCHBISHOPS OF CANTERBURY AND YORK

THIRD EDITION

LONGMANS, GREEN, AND CO.
39 PATERNOSTER ROW, LONDON
NEW YORK AND BOMBAY
1898

All rights reserved

CONTENTS

	PAGE
INTRODUCTION	1
THE POPE'S AUTHORITY TO DETERMINE THE QUESTION . . .	2
CAUSES OF THE BULL.	3
CHARACTER OF THE PREVIOUS INQUIRY	8
EVIDENCE AGAINST ANGLICAN ORDERS PASSED OVER IN THE BULL	9
EVIDENCE INVESTIGATED :	10
Extrinsic Reasons for the Decision	10
a. Anglican Orders rejected under Mary.	10
b. Anglican Orders rejected in the Gordon case . . .	19
Intrinsic Reasons for the Decision	23
Statement of Principles to be applied:—Catholic doctrine on the Real Presence—Catholic doctrine on the Sacrifice of the Mass—Catholic doctrine on the Priesthood—A digression on Transubstantiation—Catholic doctrine on the Essentials of an Ordinal—Catholic doctrine on the Intention of the Minister	23
Statement of defects found in the Anglican Ordinal and its administration. (1) The Essential Form not definite. (2) The Rite as a whole does not express the Catholic doctrine. (3) The Intention unsuited . . .	34
a. Defect of Intention (treated first for convenience' sake) .	35
b. The defect in the Essential Form	35
The *Form* of 1552 does not signify definitely . .	36
The additions in 1662 useless	38
Other prayers in the rite of 1552 do not supply deficiency	38
Objection considered (Ancient Forms not definite—National Churches may compose their own Forms) . .	41
Answer—National Churches can claim no such power .	42
Type of all the Forms acknowledged by the Church definite and identical . . ;	44
A strange misconception in the Archbishops' *Responsio*	45
A further objection: Do the terms 'bishop,' 'priest,' signify definitely ?	47

	PAGE
c. Defect in the general character of the Anglican Rite	49
The Anglican *Rite as a whole* does not signify the conveyance of the Priesthood	49
Omissions and changes in the Ordinal	51
Omissions and changes in the Communion Service	54
What did the authors of the Ordinal intend?	54
Who were the authors of the Ordinal?	55
Cranmer's doctrine on the Real Presence	57
Cranmer's doctrine on the Sacrifice of the Mass	61
Cranmer's doctrine on the Christian Priesthood	62
Doctrine of Cranmer's Colleagues	63
Destruction of Altars	64
The doctrine of the Articles	65
Cranmer's metaphorical use of the terms 'Real Presence,' 'Sacrifice' and 'Priesthood'	67
Subsequent Anglican writers in agreement with Cranmer	73
Waterland quoted	74
Cardinal Newman's estimate of the teaching of the great Anglican divines	75
Conclusion drawn	77
What is the doctrine of the *Responsio* on the Sacrifice and Priesthood?	78
Question put to the Archbishops	81
The doctrine of the Orientals on the Sacrifice and Priesthood	82
CONCLUDING WORDS	82

APPENDICES.

I. THE FACULTIES OF JULIUS III.	85
II. THE INSTRUCTION FOR THE ARMENIANS OF EUGENIUS IV.	86
III. THE RESOLUTION IN THE ABYSSINIAN CASE OF 1704	89
IV. THE ESSENTIAL FORMS OF WESTERN AND EASTERN ORDINATION RITES	93
V. THE DOCTRINE OF CRANMER'S COLLEAGUES ON THE MASS	98
VI. THE DOCTRINE OF THE LATER ANGLICAN DIVINES ON THE HOLY EUCHARIST AS A SACRAMENT AND A SACRIFICE	102
VII. THE DOCTRINE ON THE HOLY EUCHARIST OF THE SYNOD OF BETHLEHEM	116
VIII. LIST OF BOOKS AND PAMPHLETS ON ANGLICAN ORDERS	121

A LETTER

TO THE

ANGLICAN ARCHBISHOPS

1. INTRODUCTION.

Most Reverend Lords,

At the beginning of last March your Graces' 'Reply to the Papal Bull on Anglican Orders' was put into our hands. During the intervening months we have had leisure to study its contents, to observe the way in which it has been understood and accepted or rejected by the other prelates of your Communion, and in particular to learn whether the Lambeth Conference would accord to it the sanction of its adhesion. The time, therefore, seems now to have arrived when we should send you our reply. You will not be surprised at receiving a reply from us, for your Letter was 'addressed to the whole body of Bishops of the Catholic Church,' of which Church we are the appointed representatives in this country. We are moved, however, to write, not merely by the wish to acknowledge a Letter addressed to us, but much more by another cause of far greater importance. We have observed that many misconceptions have gathered round the Papal Bull, both as regards the motives which induced Leo XIII. to deal with the subject at all, and as regards the grounds on which the Bull rests its actual decision; and these misconceptions, if you will permit us to say so, underlie most of the arguments in your *Responsio*. You will agree with us that, whatever else there may be to divide us, it is a pity that we should be still further divided by pure misconceptions, especially when the effect of them is to cause a measure inspired by the purest spirit of good will to be misconstrued into an act of wanton offensiveness. May we, therefore, trust that 'in the desire to pursue peace and unity,' which you so earnestly assure us is yours no less than Leo XIII.'s, you will consider carefully what we have now to say, and will co-operate with us in our endeavour that his intentions and arguments may at least be rightly understood? May we trust also that you will give us credit for the real dispositions in which we write, and will not suspect us of motives so unseemly as those of a mere party feeling or a desire for controversial victory?

2. THE POPE'S AUTHORITY TO DETERMINE THE QUESTION.

We will begin by claiming for Leo XIII. that he has exercised only his lawful authority in deciding this controversy about Anglican Orders. We are aware that the claim will be denied by the majority of those who belong to your Communion, although some among them readily acknowledge that the Pope represents the highest religious authority in Christendom. But we will put it to you in this way. If he does possess any authority over the Church, and is capable of passing final judgment in appeal upon any question, surely it must be upon so elementary, so practical, so vital a question as the valid administration of sacraments. On the other hand, if he be not capable of giving a final judgment on such a matter, who else in the world can be capable of giving one? And if no one can give a final judgment as to what is and what is not valid administration of a sacrament, as to what is and what is not the Christian Priesthood and Sacrifice, in what a condition of inextricable chaos has Christ left His Church! In short, to deny Leo XIII.'s competency to define the conditions of a valid sacrament is to strike at the very roots of the sacramental system. For if there be no authority on earth capable of deciding so fundamental a point, how can we continue to attach vital importance to the sacraments, or to regard them as stable rites of divine institution on the due observance of which the maintenance of our spiritual life depends?

3. CAUSES OF THE BULL.

Next, as regards the causes which led the Holy See thus to deal with this question afresh.

There are times when for their own personal guidance Catholic Bishops feel the necessity of petitioning the Holy See for a judgment on the Orders of converts from the ranks of some non-Catholic ministry. It is a necessity which flows at once from the duty of guarding the sacraments against the risk of sacrilegious reiteration on the one hand and of invalid administration on the other; for in a matter of such grave importance, not only to the locality in which the convert is to minister, but likewise to the entire Catholic Church, it is for the Supreme Pontiff, and not for any lesser authority, to decide on the course to be pursued.

On all previous occasions when Anglican **Orders have** been examined at Rome the end in view has been of this nature. But in the present instance it has been otherwise. **We,** the Catholic Bishops of England, felt ourselves to **be** sufficiently guided **by the former decisions of** the Holy See, as well as **by its** unvarying sanction of **our** practice during the last three centuries. Hence we had not in any way sought, for **the** satisfaction of any doubts of our own, this new inquiry which has led to **the** *Apostolicæ Curæ*. It was in the hope of satisfying the minds of certain members of your own Communion that the inquiry was instituted; and, although we had not ourselves taken any steps to obtain it, as soon as **it was** solicited by others we confess to having been **most** anxious that for their sakes it should be conceded, and **conducted** with the **utmost care and** diligence; **for we** held **it to be of importance to** destroy if possible **the false** impression **that in a** matter affecting the *status* of your Communion the Holy See was unwilling to face the evidence with candour and **justice.**

We are aware, of course, that an entirely different account of the recent events has been suggested by writers on your side. It has been stated that the members of your Communion, being perfectly satisfied **with** their Orders, were indifferent to their recognition or non-recognition **at Rome**; that accordingly none of them had ever **asked or** thought of asking the **Holy See to** reconsider its existing practice; and **that,** in the absence alike of any domestic need among ourselves **for a** new pronouncement and of any request for one made by **you,** what has happened can only be regarded **as** a gratuitous **blow** directed against your religious feelings. This **is** indeed **a** hard thing to insinuate against a Pope like Leo XIII., and one from which his consistent attitude throughout his Pontificate towards the separated communities should surely have availed to protect him. Still, as the insinuation has been made, we must endeavour to show how unjustifiable it is, and in this endeavour at least we feel confident that we shall have your sympathy.

The Pope has been appointed by the Lord of all men to an office which embraces all men within its merciful scope. He must therefore be free, whenever he judges it opportune, to speak out on the subject of his charge, and to address not only Catholics but others also, to whatever class or section of mankind they may belong. Nor when such occasions arise can it be reasonably demanded of him that he should keep silence until those he desires to address have first approached him with their solicitations. In fact, however, in the present instance Leo XIII. was approached by those who claimed to speak, if not for the entire Anglican body, at least for a numerous section of its members. They assured him there was a widespread opinion among you that our practice of reordaining convert clergymen was an imputation on your Church which had not originated in any due inquiry, but rested on historical assumptions which could no longer be sustained. They told him they felt strongly on the matter, in the belief that you were being treated with a manifest disregard for truth and justice; and they urged that the effect was to nourish prejudices against the Holy See most injurious to the cause of Christian reunion.

The Pope was touched by the earnestness of their appeal, and determined that he would do all within his power to remove obstacles from the path to reunion, and convince you of the friendliness of his attitude. Accordingly he directed that a fresh inquiry into the character of your Orders should be made, and made with the greatest thoroughness and impartiality; so that if it should appear that an injustice was really being done it might be rectified forthwith. It was in this manner that the train of events originated which in due course led to the *Apostolicæ Curæ*; and, surely, there is nothing here which can be rightly construed into a wanton attack, or even into an unfriendly act. The Pope's desire was so far as possible to please, but he could not be expected to grant what an inquiry had shown could not be granted without sacrilege. The only course was to announce the result of the inquiry, and to announce it in terms of sympathy and cordiality. And this is what he did in the recent Bull.

Should you, however, question the correctness of this account, we will not ask you to believe anything on our personal testimony, since we can direct you to the testimony of notorious facts and to the published statements of Leo XIII. himself. It is matter of common knowledge that some members of your Communion allied themselves with some members of ours in order to work for corporate reunion, and that they deemed it necessary for the success of their movement that we should cease to reject your Orders. To assist them in bringing this to pass they caused a treatise containing an effective statement of your arguments to be written in Latin and circulated among our theologians and ecclesiastical rulers abroad. At Rome they were especially assiduous in distributing copies, and they presented one to the Holy Father himself. What other object could this propagandism be supposed to have save that of inducing the Pope to do exactly what he has done? It was obvious that so serious an alteration in our practice could not be initiated save under his sanction and directions, nor could he be expected to sanction it except after a searching inquiry into its lawfulness; nor could he, when the inquiry to which all were looking had been concluded, withhold its decision from the world without exposing his action to dangerous misconstructions.

We have undertaken to refer you to the Pope's own testimony to this sequence of events. Have you noticed that in the Bull itself he recounts the causes which led to its publication, and that he gives exactly those which we have stated?

For some time [he says], and in these last years especially, a controversy has sprung up as to whether the sacred Orders conferred according to the Edwardine Ordinal possessed the nature and effect of a Sacrament; those in favour of the absolute validity or of a doubtful validity being not only certain Anglican writers, but some few Catholics, mostly non-English. The consideration of the excellency of the Christian priesthood moved Anglican writers in this matter, desirous as they were that their own people should not lack the twofold power over the Body of Christ. Catholic writers were impelled by a wish to smooth the way for the return of Anglicans to holy unity. *Both indeed thought* that in view of studies brought up to the level of recent research, and of new documents rescued from oblivion, it was not inopportune to re-examine the question by Our authority. And We, *not disregarding such desires and opinions*, and above all obeying the dictates of Apostolic charity, have considered that nothing should be left untried that might in any way tend to preserve souls from injury or procure their advantage.

The other statement of Leo XIII. on this subject is to be found in his letter to the Cardinal Archbishop of Paris recommending the discontinuance of a certain magazine. It was dated November 5, 1896, and was published some months later in the *Acta Sanctæ Sedis*.[1] We learn from it, not only that he had been asked to institute the late inquiry, but the pain and surprise he has felt at the subsequent action of the applicants. The passage which concerns us is the following:

> Whereas certain Englishmen who dissent from the Catholic religion appeared to be inquiring of Us in the spirit of sincerity what was the truth **about their** ordinations, but received this same truth, when **We had declared it to them** before God, in **a** very different spirit, **it** plainly **follows** . . .

You will not disbelieve this testimony of the Venerable Pontiff on a matter which lay so well within his knowledge, but you may wonder that we have dwelt on it at such length, seeing that in your own Letter it has no place save by way of transient allusion in a single clause (Section I.). We have dwelt on it because the misconstruction is still industriously propagated, and has tended more than anything else to convert into an instrument of embitterment what Leo XIII. intended as a message of peace.

4. CHARACTER OF THE PREVIOUS INQUIRY.

So much as to the origin of the inquiry. But the notion has also been disseminated that, when made, it was not conducted with impartiality or thoroughness. You yourselves seem to be under this impression, and say that what was done 'would seem to have been done in appearance rather than in reality' (Section VIII.). But this also we must set down as a misconception

---

[1] Vol. xvi. p. 305. It may be read also in Appendix I. of Father Brandi's *Roma e Canterbury*.

calculated to do harm. That in its earlier stages the inquiry was thorough and impartial has been acknowledged by your own writers in terms of cordiality which are still on record;[1] and the method adopted from the first was continued faithfully to the end. The materials bearing on every department of the subject, which had been furnished and sifted by the representatives of both sides during the Preparatory Commission, were passed on to the Judicial Commission of the Holy Office and then to the Pope. It was only after this collection and weighing of a large mass of evidence that the final judgment was formed. Proof of this could be offered without difficulty. As, however, your writers have been led to suspect the adequacy of the inquiry, not by any knowledge they possess of the facts, but, as it appears to us, solely by their persuasion that the decision reached is wrong and the reasons offered for it unsound, we will pass at once to these reasons and your criticisms upon them.

5. EVIDENCE PASSED OVER BY THE BULL.

One word, first, as to some reasons which the Bull passes over. To these you allude in Section IV., where you assume that the Bull means to reject as 'errors and fallacies' certain reasons to which it does not appeal, although they have been urged by Catholic writers as telling with more or less probability against your Orders. You are referring, of course, to the doubts expressed about Barlow's and Parker's consecrations, and to the arguments founded on the omission

---

[1] See *Church Times* for April 24, 1896, in a Presidential Address to the English Church Union; and for May 8, 1896, in a letter quoted from the *Cowley Magazine*.

of delivery of the instruments in the rite. Here is another misconception. The Bull neither pronounces nor insinuates any judgment, favourable or unfavourable, on the value of these reasons. It merely passes them over as not requiring to be examined, since, even apart from them, the invalidity of your Orders was decisively proved.

6. EVIDENCE INVESTIGATED.

In Section V. you come to the reasons which were examined and on which the condemnation rests—the authoritative character of the practice hitherto followed, and the defects found in your Ordination rite itself after a fresh study of its language and history.

Of these arguments you tell us that you do not attach much importance to the first, and, of course, if you refuse to acknowledge the teaching authority of the Holy See, you cannot be prepared to accept as final its past decisions in a matter so closely concerning you. Still you will recognise that Leo XIII. could not fail to lay stress on them, and at the very least you will allow that it is according to common usage for a tribunal about to decide a case brought under its notice, to inquire carefully into its past decisions in like cases, particularly when it has been assured that they were based only on disproved assumptions.

7. EXTRINSIC REASONS FOR THE DECISION.
(a) ANGLICAN ORDERS REJECTED UNDER MARY.

In the past, Leo XIII. tells us, the Holy See has given its approbation to the reordination of clergymen leaving your ranks for ours, both virtually by permitting the practice to continue, and expressly on more than one occasion. In particular the Bull calls attention to the directions given to Pole when he was engaged in reconciling the kingdom under Mary, and to the decision given in the Gordon case in 1704. To the exposition of these cases you devote two sections of your Reply (Sections VI., VII.). We should prefer not to enlarge on this branch of the question, partly because it is less satisfactory to spend time in vindicating the character of decisions the authority of which, whatever be their tenor, you are not prepared to accept, and still more because a full discussion of these cases runs necessarily into technical details not easy for the mass of readers to follow. Still, as you challenge so decidedly Leo XIII.'s treatment of these two cases, we will endeavour to explain and vindicate it as simply as we can, referring you for a fuller handling of the various points to the writers named in the footnote.[1]

To instruct us as to the course followed in the reconciliation under Mary, there is extant a series of authentic instruments in which, among other matters, the mode for dealing with Edwardine Orders is clearly laid down; and it is to these that Leo XIII. has referred. The series comprises (1) the Letter of Julius III. (*Dudum dum charissima*) to Cardinal Pole, dated March 8, 1554, in which the terms of a previous Letter of August 5, 1553, are recited, and the faculties therein contained are renewed and enlarged; (2) a set of Letters written by Pole to his suffragans, and subdelegating to them a portion of the aforesaid faculties,

---

[1] See the articles in the *Tablet* of July 10 and 17, 1897, by Monsignor Moyes; Father Brandi's *Last Word on Anglican Ordinations* and his *Roma e Canterbury*, Terza edizione; and for the text of the various official documents, see Father A. S. Barnes's *The Popes and the Ordinal*, and the Church Historical Society's *Treatise on the Bull 'Apostolicæ Curæ.'*

from among which Letters the *Apostolicæ Curæ* quotes a portion of that addressed, under date January 29, 1555, to the Bishop of Norwich; (3) the Bull of Paul IV. (*Præclara charissimi*), dated June 20, 1555, in which that Pope, responding to an application from Pole, ratifies what had been done by the latter and his suffragans in the exercise of their faculties, and makes their acts his own; (4) the Brief (*Regimini universalis*) of the same Pontiff, dated October 30, 1555, in which he corrects a misunderstanding which had arisen as to the meaning of a phrase in the *Præclara charissimi*, a misunderstanding bearing on this very question of Edwardine Orders. To which four documents may be added, although it is not cited in the recent Bull, a document found among the Vatican Archives[1] which gives a Summary of the concessions Pole desired to have ratified in the *Præclara charissimi*, and the Bull is found to correspond with this Summary in all particulars. It is clear that these several documents require to be read together and used to explain one another, and this is how Leo XIII. has dealt with them.

What we find in these various documents is as follows. (1) The **Papal** Letter **of** March 8, 1554, in the part quoted from **the previous** Letter, distinguishes the persons at that time *de facto* ministering in the country into two classes—'those who had been rightly and properly promoted or ordained before their lapse into this manner of heresy,' and 'those who had not been promoted'—allowing the former to use their Orders after **due** dispensation from censures incurred, and the latter **to receive** all Orders, the priesthood included, if found **fit** and worthy. (2) **The latter** part of this same Letter of March 8, referring evidently to the same class

---

[1] The text may be read in *Roma e Canterbury*, p. 56.

which had previously been called 'persons not promoted,' speaks of them as persons needing ' dispensations in regard to Orders which they had *never* or *badly* received,' or in regard ' to the gift of consecration which they had received . . . *defectively* [*minus rite*], and *without the observance of the accustomed form of the Church.*' (3) **Pole's** Letter to the **Bishop** of Norwich empowers him to permit, after dispensation from censures, the use of their existing Orders 'even **to** those who had received them from heretical and schismatical **Bishops,** and even though they had received them *defectively* [*minus rite*] *provided the form and intention of the Church had been observed* in the conveyance of them.' (4) The Bull *Præclara charissimi*, **while** giving **full force** and approbation to what **Pole had done, and,** therefore, inclusively to his directions to disregard as 'never received' Orders which had been imparted by a form and intention other than 'the form and intention of the Church,' cautiously adds a further limiting clause to guard against another possible source of invalidity which Pole's commissions to his suffragans had not directly specified—viz. that if **any** person should have been promoted **by** the use of a rite, however valid in itself, but administered by '*a Bishop or Archbishop not duly and rightly ordained,*' such Orders should be similarly disregarded, **and** the holders ordained afresh by their own ordinaries. (5) The Brief of October 30 explains to us that by ' Bishops not duly and **rightly** ordained ' were meant those, and those only, '**who** had not been ordained and consecrated **by** the *form of the Church.*' (6) The Summary, not mentioned in the *Apostolicæ Curæ*, is useful on account of the following clause : ' Dispensations [granted by the Most Rev. Legate for which ratification is sought] with ecclesiastical persons, whether secular or belonging to the different [religious] Orders, so that they may be promoted both in *Orders* and in benefices *invalidly* [*nulliter*] obtained during the schism.'[1]

When all these passages are read together, it becomes perfectly clear that there were certain persons ministering at the time, as bishops, priests, or deacons, who might desire to be reconciled, but whose Orders were accounted invalid, and that what had made their Orders invalid was their derivation from a certain form or rite which had been substituted in the place of the 'form of the Church.' Now, by the 'form of the Church' was obviously meant the form prescribed in the Pontifical, in one or other of the practically identical texts which had till recent times been in use in the country; by the rival form, therefore, could only have been meant the Edwardine form, which everyone knew had been substituted for the Catholic Church's own established form. This is what the Bull *Apostolicæ Curæ* has inferred, very reasonably pointing out that to suppose that any other than the Edwardine form was intended, would be to suppose that the Papal and other Letters bore no reference to the actual needs of the persons to whom they were sent.

Although the meaning and purport of these authentic instruments appear to be sufficiently clear from their text, it may not be amiss to remind you of the evidence which, by showing that Edwardine Orders were in fact treated as invalid by Pole and his colleagues, affords

---

[1] It is suggested in the *Responsio* (Section VI.) that, besides the faculties of Julius III. mentioned by Leo XIII., there were others 'granted to Pole after 5 August 1553 and before 8 March 1554,' and that 'without these (other) **faculties** '—which, however, the Bull *Apostolicæ Curæ* disregards—' the "**rules** of action " which Pole was to observe are imperfectly known.' On this point see Appendix I.

confirmatory proof that this was what they understood the documents to require. We may call your attention to two contemporary writers who tell us plainly that Edwardine Orders were treated as invalid.

One is Bonner, who, in his *Profitable and Necessary Doctrine*, in his section *On the Sacrament of Orders*, says:

Therefore the late made ministers in the time of the schism, *in their newly devised ordination*, having **no authority at** all given **them** to offer in the Mass the Body and **Blood of Our** Saviour Christ, but both they so ordered (or rather *disordered*), **and** their schismatical orderers also, utterly despising and impugning, not only the Oblation **of the** Sacrifice of the Mass, but also the Real Presence **of the Body** and Blood of **our** Saviour Christ in the Sacrament of the **Altar.** Therefore I **say** that **all** such ... most pitifully beguiled the people **of** this realm who *by this means were defrauded of the most Blessed Body* **and** *Blood of our Saviour Christ* ... and also of the *Sacrifice of the Mass* ... and seeing that every man **(be he** never so simple) **may** sufficiently hereby perceive how *these late counterfeited ministers* have in so weighty a matter deceived the people ... you **may** thereby consider both what thanks you owe to Almighty God **who** hath *restored unto you the right use of the Sacraments* again, and also how much you ought to esteem *the right priesthood now brought home again,* by which as an ordinary means God worketh His graces amongst you.

Bonner here calls the Edwardine clergy 'disordered,' not ordered, **and** therefore 'counterfeit **ministers**,' who, having no power to effect the same, have defrauded the people of Our Lord's Body and Blood and of the Sacrifice of the Mass, **which,** however, the 'right priesthood' had since restored to them. What else can this mean save that the holders of Edwardine Orders were either **ordained** afresh or expelled from the ministry of the Altar **altogether**?

The other witness has used language which is cited in your Graces' Letter, although you do not seem to have perceived its true significance.

'In the late days of the Popery' (writes Pilkington, one of Elizabeth's Protestant Bishops) 'our Holy Bishops called before them all such as were made ministers without such greasing, and blessed them with the Pope's blessing, anointed them, and then all was perfect; they might sacrifice for quick and dead, but not marry in no case.'[1] Pilkington was not referring, as you suppose, to the use of a ceremony regarded as important but not essential, for he speaks of a ceremony the effect of which was to impart the power of saying Mass and to impose the obligation of celibacy. He was referring, therefore, to absolute ordinations, although he described them by a feature in the Catholic rite which best lent itself to his ridicule. We have it therefore on his authority that all the ministers in Edwardine Orders who were taken on by Mary's prelates went through a ceremony of Catholic reordination; and as Pilkington had been in England at the time of the reconciliation under Mary, he was a competent witness to those facts, and had no motive for misstating them.

We may also cite, in further confirmation of Leo XIII.'s contention, the facts which a recent search among your Episcopal Registers has ascertained. There are entered, it seems, in the Marian Registers of the dioceses of London and Oxford alone, thirteen or fourteen names of persons then ordained, who in the Edwardine Registers are entered as having previously received Anglican Orders. Seeing that the Edwardine clergy for the most part were ardently attached to their

[1] *Expositions on the Prophet Aggeus*, ii. 10-14. Pilkington's *Works*. Parker Society's edition.

anti-Catholic beliefs, were married men, and were disqualified in many ways for the Catholic ministry, this is a large number out of a total of one hundred clergy and six bishops whose names are recorded as having received Orders through the use of the new Ordinal. And it is only your Graces' want of familiarity with our beliefs and feelings which has led you to suppose that these reordinations, which you acknowledge to be such, could have been 'voluntary,' or given in deference to the chance feelings of the individual applicant or prelate. To us who know the sense of responsibility with which Catholic Bishops watch over the Sacrament of Holy Orders, it is simply inconceivable that the Marian prelates could have acted in so light and irrational a manner. On the contrary, we understand at once that, if thirteen or fourteen were reordained, all others who were similarly situated must have been reordained likewise, or have retired into private life.

Even this is not all the evidence adducible to prove that we have rightly stated the opinion of the Marian authorities. There yet remains the argument arising out of the course followed in degrading or not degrading the Edwardine clergy when condemned for heresy. Thus Cranmer, Ridley, and Latimer, who were all consecrated by the Catholic rite, were degraded from the episcopate; whereas Hooper and Ferrar, who had been consecrated bishops by the new method but ordained priests by the old, were degraded only from the priesthood—which must mean that their episcopal orders were treated as non-existent. Several similar cases are on record out of which we can construct a table showing that, when ordination was by the Catholic rite, degradation from the order thus received was always part of the sentence, whilst, when it was by the

Edwardine rite, no mention is made of any degradation to be inflicted.[1] Bradford's case is of special interest. There is extant among the British Museum MSS. the original instrument, containing his sentence of condemnation.[2] He had been ordained deacon by Ridley according to the Edwardine rite, and had held the living of Kentish Town. Yet in this sentence of condemnation, not only is he called 'John Bradford, *layman*,' but the clause ' that he must be degraded and deposed from every **priestly** order according to the sacred canons,' which had been inserted by the engrossing clerk, is scored through. Nor is there any substituted clause to require his degradation from the diaconate. He was not to be degraded at all, which must mean that there was considered to be in him no character from which he could be degraded. Moreover John Taylor, John Hooper, and John Harley, the **Edwardine** Bishops of Lincoln, Worcester and Gloucester, and Hereford, according to Wharton[3] are entered in the Canterbury Register expressly as deprived *propter nullitatem consecrationis*.

The inquiry into the proceedings under Mary was useful in showing that—contrary to what had been alleged on your side, and is even repeated in your Reply—the practice of rejecting your Orders did not spring up gradually and without authorisation, but goes back to the time when they first came under

---

[1] For Cranmer and Latimer, Hooper and Ferrar, see Foxe *in loc.*, and for Ridley, Foxe as corrected by Estcourt, pp. 53, 54. Compare also **ap. Foxe** *in loc.*, the accounts of Rogers, Atholle, Samnell, Flower, **Whittle,** Taylor of Hadley Rough, Yeoman, with those of Philpott, **Bland,** Marsh, Drakes, Tims, Simpson. For the evidence that Ferrar was consecrated after the new fashion, see Estcourt, p. 54, and his **App.** viii.

[2] *Harleian,* 421, fol. **46.**

[3] See footnote in Pocock's *Burnet,* ii **p. 441.**

notice. It has been demonstrated that this **practice was even then formally authorised**, and that it was based on a **systematic examination of the Ordinal**; for that your Ordinal was itself then examined is proved not only by the **tenor** of the Papal directions in the various Letters cited, but by the **discovery in the Vatican Archives** of a descriptive summary of its **text among** the papers relating to the reconciliation.[1]

8. EXTRINSIC REASONS—
(b) THE GORDON CASE.

The inquiry into the Gordon decision of 1704 has carried us a step further, for it furnishes **not merely** the broad fact that a fresh investigation then took place, and led to an unhesitating decision, **but** also the grounds on which this new decision turned, which prove to have been, not as was represented, mere fables and false assumptions, but reasons solid enough to stand the test of recent research. They are in fact the same in substance as those which—as the result of the late investigation—are set forth in the *Apostolicæ Curæ*.

It is important [says the Bull] to observe that—although Gordon himself, whose case it was, and some of the consultors, had adduced, as amongst the reasons calling for a decree of nullity, the ordination of Parker according to their own ideas about it—in the delivery of the decision *this reason was altogether set aside*, as documents of incontestable authenticity prove. Nor in pronouncing the decision was weight given to any other reason than the 'defect of form and intention'; and in order that the judgment concerning this form might be more certain and complete, precaution was taken that *a copy of the Anglican Ordinal should be submitted* to examination, and that *with it should be collated the Ordination forms gathered together*

---

[1] *Arch. Vatic. Nuntiatura di Inghilterra*, m. 103. Cp. *Bibliotheca Pia*, 240.

from the **Eastern and** *Western rites.* . . . It is important to bear in mind that *this judgment* **was in no** *wise determined by the omission* **of** *the delivery of the* **instruments,** for in such a case, **according to** established custom, the **direction** would have been **to repeat the** Ordination conditionally.

These words seem plain enough. We confess, therefore, to some surprise that, in spite of them, you should continue to suggest, in the Appendix to your *Responsio*, that the Holy Office 'accepted Gordon's assertions on that subject' (*i.e.* on the character of your Ordinal) and that 'the documents of incontestable authenticity,' of which Leo XIII. speaks, 'really say nothing about the kind of defect, since it is only conjecturally inferred.' We are now, however, able to direct your attention to evidence in confirmation of the Holy Father's testimony, which you can hardly resist.

Father Brandi has published some of the 'documents of incontestable authenticity' in his *Roma e Canterbury*. Among them is a letter from Mgr. Tanari, addressed to Cardinal Casanata, and dated May 4, 1685. Mgr. Tanari was at the time Internunzio at Brussels, and had apparently been commissioned to obtain a printed copy of the Anglican Ordinal, for the use of the Congregation in the case of that year which the Bull mentions. In his letter Tanari tells us that he sends such a copy therewith, and attached to the letter in the Archives of the Congregation is the copy in question. It is a copy of the entire rite, not, as has been suggested, of a portion only. The members of the recent Roman Commission had it in their hands, and Father Brandi has given a facsimile of the first page. Needless to say, it proves to be the page containing the Preface to your Ordinal, and a portion of the rite for making deacons. This shows that the entire Ordinal in its most authentic form, and not merely the rite for any single Order, was under the consideration of the judges of 1704. The collection also contains the *votum* and *relatio* of Cardinal Casanata, the Cardinal deputed to report in the case of 1685, the case to which Leo XIII. refers as having preceded the Gordon case by a short interval, and as having furnished many papers which were used again when the Gordon case came on. These two papers of Casanata's, together with Mgr. Tanari's letter and the copy of your Ordinal, were among the documents thus used again in 1704. Casanata's *votum* and *relatio* are of interest, because they are 'documents of incontestable authenticity' which show, as Leo XIII. has said, that the want of delivery of the instruments in your Ordinal was not the reason of its condemnation at that time. In the *votum* Casanata thus expresses himself:

That these forms are insufficient for the ordination of priests and bishops is effectually proved by the following fundamental reason. The Sacraments only operate what they signify either expressly or at least implicitly. Now the words of the said forms do not signify in any manner [*in nessuna maniera*] the most essential power of the priest and bishop, that is, the power of offering sacrifice and consecrating the Body of Christ. Hence they do not operate, or confer such a power; all the more that there is wanting in them the delivery of the instruments of sacrifice, which is used in the Latin Church to signify the said power. . . . It is true that in their ordination there is imposition of hands, and that many theologians, appealing to the use of the Greeks and other reasons, hold that imposition of hands suffices without the delivery of the instruments. But apart from the fact that this cannot be said with certainty, as long as the Church, or a notable part of the same, has assigned the said delivery as the matter in her Ordinations, and has in this manner attached to it, so to speak, the significa- tion of the power of sacrifice, which determination many con- sider that Christ has left her free to make—apart from this, I say, the imposition of hands is an ambiguous sign, which needs to be determined to signify a particular power either by the accompanying words or by other circumstances. Now in the Ordinations of the English the imposition of hands is determined to the **power** of remitting sin and not to the **power of** offering **sacrifice**, which is rather excluded, at least, **by the intention.**

Here we see that Casanata refers indeed to the omission of the delivery of the instruments in your Ordinal, and deduces an argument from it. But this argument is not that your Ordinal, being one in which delivery **of** the instruments has no place, belongs to a class of Ordinals which are certainly invalid. On the contrary, he expressly acknowledges that there are Ordinals without delivery of the instruments which the Church has never hesitated to treat as valid. And although he reminds the Congregation that in the Western Church this ceremony may possibly **be** essential, by reason of **the Church's** adoption of it as her authorised mode of signifying the sacramental effect, still he is careful not to rest his absolute rejection of your Ordinal on this. His main argument, on which alone he rests his conclusion that Gordon **must be reordained, is** that, whereas imposition **of hands is of itself an** ambiguous sign, there is nothing **in the Ordinations of the** English by which its ambiguity **is** determined **to** the power of offering sacrifice—neither the accompanying words, nor **the delivery of sacrificial** instruments, nor anything **else, whether '** explicit or implicit.' In the face, then, **of this** passage **from** Casanata we hardly think you will continue to suggest that the Gordon decision was based either on ignorance of the text of your Ordinal, or on obsolete ideas **about** the necessity of a certain ceremony. On the contrary, you will recognise that the reasons on **which** that decision was based are identical with those which in a more developed form are set forth in the *Apostolicæ Curæ*.

9. INTRINSIC REASONS FOR THE DECISION.

We come now to the intrinsic reasons which Leo XIII. indicates as having compelled him to reject your Orders—the defects of *form* and of *intention* which he finds in them. And here we may begin by reminding you that, in acceding to the requests of those who asked him for a fresh inquiry, he did not dream of opening an inquiry into the truth of such Catholic doctrines as those of the sacrifice and the priesthood. These for the Catholic Church are matters not admitting of doubt or dispute. The only question which he could consent to entertain was as to whether your Ordinal fulfils the conditions which in the judgment of the Catholic Church are indispensable for the conferring the kind of priesthood and episcopate in which she believes. If you hold a different doctrine from hers in regard to these Orders, we must leave you to settle for yourselves what rites are suitable, and what not, to make a minister of the Anglican Communion. But if some of your people come to us and seek to have their Orders recognised by the Catholic Church, then it is by our doctrines and requirements that the question must be determined.

10. STATEMENT OF PRINCIPLES TO BE APPLIED.

This being so, and much misconception prevailing on the subject, we will begin what we have to say about the intrinsic reasons by a brief doctrinal statement, in which we desire to call particular attention to the intimate connection between the four doctrines of the Real Presence, the Sacrifice, the Priesthood, and the requisite character of the Ordinal.

11. CATHOLIC DOCTRINE ON THE REAL PRESENCE

By the doctrine of the Real Presence we mean that by the words of consecration there are made present under the appearances of bread and wine the true Body and Blood of Jesus Christ, and likewise—since in the living Christ soul and body are inseparable—His Soul and Divinity. We say that His true Body is present, meaning that what is present on the altar is not some symbol of the Body of Christ, but His Body itself, the very Body which hung on the Cross. This also is what we mean by the word 'really': namely, that His Body is not present merely figuratively, as if only a figure of itself were what is present really; nor merely virtually, as though some effect of its virtue and power, such as grace, were what is present really; but that the Body itself is present. We further call the Real Presence an Objective Presence, meaning that the Body of Christ is not merely present to faith, as an idea is present to the thinking mind, but is present on the altar, so as to be there quite independently of any action of the believing mind upon it. Our theologians also speak of this Presence at times as a 'spiritual' presence, not using the term 'spiritual' in the sense in which the 'spirit' is opposed to the 'letter,' or the thing signified to its sign, but meaning to denote by it that the Body of Christ, although in itself a body, not a spirit, enjoys nevertheless a mode of existence natural not to a body but to a spirit—that mode of existence, in fact, which, according to St. Paul, is granted to a risen body

(1 Cor. xv. 44), and delivers it **from many of** the limitations to which a material body is naturally subject.

Such is the Catholic doctrine. We do not deny that it affirms a stupendous mystery of existence, nor do we profess to explain how such a mystery is possible. We are content to adhere faithfully to our Lord's own teaching, as **preserved to** us in the language of Holy Scripture and the Tradition of the Catholic Church.

12. CATHOLIC DOCTRINE ON THE SACRIFICE OF THE MASS.

The Mass, according to Catholic **doctrine, is a** commemoration of the Sacrifice of the Cross, for as often as we celebrate it 'we show the Lord's death till He come.' At the same time it is not a bare commemoration of that other sacrifice, since it is also itself a true sacrifice in the strict sense of **the term.** It is a true sacrifice, because it has all the essentials of a true sacrifice: its Priest, Jesus Christ using the ministry of an earthly representative; its Victim, Jesus Christ, truly present under the appearances of bread and wine; its **Sacrificial Offering, the mystic rite of** consecration. And it commemorates the Sacrifice of the Cross, because, whilst its **Priest is** the Priest of Calvary, its Victim the Victim of Calvary, and its mode of offering a mystic representation **of** the **blood-shedding of Calvary,** the end also for which it is offered **is** to carry on the work of Calvary, by pleading for the application of **the** merits consummated on the Cross to the souls of **men.** It is in this sense that the Mass is propitiatory. To propitiate is to appease the Divine wrath by satisfaction offered and to beg mercy and forgiveness for sinners. The Sacrifice of the Cross is propitiatory in the absolute sense of the word. But the infinite treasure of merit acquired on the Cross cannot be diminished or increased by any other sacrifice. It was then offered once and for all, and there is no necessity of repeating it. That plenitude, however, of merit and satisfaction by no means excludes the continual application of such merit and satisfaction by the perpetual Sacrifice of the Mass. Thus the Sacrifice of the Mass is also propitiatory. And, as according to **Catholic** doctrine even the dead in Christ are not excluded from the benefits of this sacrifice, we call the Mass ' a propitiatory sacrifice for the living and the dead.'

Such being our doctrine of the Eucharistic Sacrifice, its essential dependence on the doctrine of the Real Objective Presence is manifest. For, if there were no power in the words of consecration to make the true Body and Blood of Christ really and objectively present on the altar, we should not have on our altars the Victim of Calvary, and without its victim the sacrifice could not subsist.

13. CATHOLIC DOCTRINE ON THE PRIESTHOOD.

Next as to our doctrine of the Priesthood. Priest and Sacrifice are correlative terms—with us at all events, and indeed with all nations, except in so far as your own Communion may be an exception. A priest is one who offers sacrifice ; and, as is the sacrifice, so is the priest. **Since,** then, our sacrifice is the Sacrifice **of** the Mass, our priest is one appointed and empowered to offer up that sacrifice ; one, therefore, who has received from God the power, by means of the words of consecration, to cause the Body and Blood of Christ to become present under the appearances of bread and wine, and to offer them up sacrificially. He may have other powers annexed to his office, as the power of forgiving sins; **and he may be** likewise charged with the duty of preaching the Word of God and exercising pastoral care over the people. But these other powers and duties are superadded and consequent. They are very suitably annexed to the priesthood, but they are not of its essence. The priest would **not have** been less a priest if they had been withheld from him, nor is he more a priest because Our Lord has thought fit to communicate them to him. He is a priest solely because he has the office and power of effecting the Real Objective Presence on the altar of the true Body and Blood of Jesus Christ, and thereby offering Him up in sacrifice.

We have spoken of the Priesthood only in the preceding paragraph, and we **may** be reminded that something should be said about the Episcopate also. But we have only to add that this priesthood ordained to offer **up** the Holy Sacrifice of the Mass has been instituted by Our Lord in two distinct degrees, of which one **possesses** the substance of the priestly power, but not its plenitude, the other both; **or**, in other words, **in** which one possesses the power to sacrifice, but that only—the other possesses not only the power of sacrifice in itself, but likewise the further power of communicating that power to others.

14. A DIGRESSION ON TRANSUBSTANTIATION.

It may have seemed to you that in this account of our doctrine of the priesthood we have been purposely avoiding the use of the term 'transubstantiation.' This is true, and we must explain why we have done so. Our doctrine of transubstantiation is not founded, as some suppose, on a philosophical theory, but on the plain meaning of the words of institution. If the words of consecration, 'This is My Body,' 'This is My Blood,' are interpreted figuratively, as they are by the Zwinglians and Calvinists, all will admit that there is no place left for a doctrine of consubstantiation, whereby bread and wine and the Body and Blood of Christ are concomitantly present. If, on the other hand, conformably with the requirements of context and of the constant Tradition of the Catholic Church, they are interpreted literally, there is still no place for a doctrine of consubstantiation, but only for one of transubstantiation. For the words declare, not that the Body and Blood of Christ are present within or beneath or by the side of the bread and wine, but that the things present before the consecrator *are themselves* the Body and Blood of Christ under the appearances of bread and wine. Now as, before the words were spoken, the things present were unquestionably mere bread and wine, and as they cannot be at one and the same time both bread and wine and also the Body and Blood of Christ, they **can** become the latter only by a change of the former into the latter, which change, since it is a change of one substance into another, the accidents or sensible qualities remaining unaffected, **is** appropriately designated 'transubstantiation.' So, **then**, whilst not denying that **Our Lord** might, had He so wished, have instituted the Sacrament in such manner **that** the bread and wine and the Body and Blood should be present concomitantly, we deny emphatically that the character of the words of institution permits us to believe that He did, and we refuse in consequence to clog our terminology with an unnecessary distinction. By the term 'transubstantiation' we mean always that supernatural act by which the Body and Blood of Christ are made present on our altars in the Mass. It is observable, too, that this is also the sense attached to the term by the general mass of Protestants, ancient and modern. When they employ it they have usually in mind the doctrine of a Real Presence wrought by the words of the priest, not the doctrine that it is wrought through a conversion of the bread and wine into the Body and Blood of Christ. This latter they as well as we take to be a necessary consequence of the former, and this is why in the writings of the Reformation period, on the Catholic and Protestant side alike—indeed, in writings on our side and yours up to the present century—the term 'transubstantiation' is the term constantly used, even when the context shows that the point directly in dispute is not as to the manner in which the Real Objective Presence is effected, but as to the doctrine of the Real Objective Presence itself.

Such being the accepted signification of the term, we should be entitled so to use it in this Letter, and likewise, when we come to examine the writings of your divines, to claim the majority of passages in which they repudiate transubstantiation as passages in which they repudiate the Real Objective Presence, and the sacrifice which is dependent on it. Still, as you dispute the correctness of this account, and as we desire to avoid all issues which are not absolutely necessary, we are refraining altogether from the use of the term 'transubstantiation,' and shall likewise refrain from laying stress on its use by your divines. We shall be able to find sufficient testimony in their writings, quite apart from their utterances about transubstantiation, to demonstrate their denial of that Real Objective Presence without which most certainly there is no possibility of a belief in such a Eucharistic Sacrifice as our priests are ordained to offer.

15. CATHOLIC DOCTRINE ON THE ESSENTIALS OF AN ORDINAL.

The way is now smoothed for understanding the doctrine of the Catholic Church as to the essentials of a valid ordination. For a valid ordination a valid *form* (or *rite*) and a proper *intention* are required.

First, then, as regards the FORM or RITE. It is the teaching of the Catholic Church that Our Lord, having established the Christian priesthood, determined that it should be perpetuated through the ages by an Apostolical Succession, those who received the gift directly from His hands transmitting it to others, who in turn should transmit it to the next generation, and so to the end; with the result that no man can be truly deemed to possess the priesthood or the episcopate who has not received it in this manner through Apostolical Succession. It is likewise the teaching of the Catholic Church that the bishop in thus transmitting his gift to others must use a rite instituted by Our Lord Himself. He must do this, because none but Our Lord could annex to a sacramental rite the power of communicating gifts so stupendous, and it was His good pleasure to institute each one of the Sacraments Himself, during His earthly life, by assigning to each the rite which, as a condition of valid administration, must always be observed. And, as our knowledge of what Our Lord instituted and prescribed in regard to the Sacraments is derived from the unfailing Tradition of the Catholic Church, it is this we must consult if we wish to learn what are the necessary elements of a valid ordination rite. The Bull itself explains to us what these essentials are, in words of which the meaning may be more fully expounded thus.

In every sacramental rite we must distinguish the part which is ESSENTIAL from that which is purely CEREMONIAL. The essential part is comparatively short, in most Sacraments very short. The distinction, however, does not turn on any question of length, but on the contents of the respective parts. The essential part must contain within itself all that is essential to the due conveyance of the grace or power attached to the Sacrament. The purely ceremonial part, on the other hand, consists merely of such elements as have been added in course of time to give fuller expression to the nature of the gift or greater solemnity to the occasion. The essential part must (1) *signify* the grace or power to be conveyed; for, as the Bull tells us, 'it is the nature of a Sacrament to signify what it effects, and to effect what it signifies.' Moreover, the signification must not be ambiguous, but (2) so far *definite* as to discriminate the grace effected from graces of a different kind; as, for instance, the graces of other Sacraments. And whereas, by the institution of Christ, there are in the essential part of each Sacrament two elements distinguishable—an appropriate ceremony, which since the twelfth or thirteenth century has been usually called the *matter*, and an accompanying form of words, which has been usually called the *form* (in the more restricted sense)[1]—(3) the definiteness of signification

---

[1] The term 'form' is sometimes used to designate the combination of words and ceremony which constitute the essential portion of the sacramental rite; sometimes in a more restricted sense to denote the words of this essential portion in contradistinction to the ceremony or 'matter'; sometimes more loosely to denote the entire rite, to the

must be chiefly sought *in the form*—since words are able to define a meaning with precision, whilst a ceremony, apart from any defining words accompanying it, can hardly be without ambiguity. That at least these three elements are by the institution of Christ essential to a valid rite is the clear teaching of Catholic Tradition, and it is as such that they are set forth by the Bull and employed as the basis of its argument. Whether it be likewise essential that either the matter or the form, or both, should have been prescribed by Our Lord *in specie* and not merely *in genere*, as the theologians say, is a question which it did not fall within the scope of the Bull to decide. It is a question, however, which will meet us again presently.

With one exception these principles apply to all the Sacraments of the Church. That one exception is Matrimony, which, being a contract, originally natural but elevated to the supernatural order, is regulated by somewhat different principles.

On the other hand, to quote from the Bull, the principles just explained 'appear still more clearly in Holy Orders, the matter of which, in so far as we have to consider it in this case, is the imposition of hands; which indeed by itself signifies nothing definite, and is equally used for several Orders and for Confirmation.' Particularly, therefore, in the rite for Holy Orders, we must look to the words accompanying the imposition of hands and ascertain whether they definitely signify, or express that which this sacrament is intended to convey—namely, 'the sacred Order of priesthood or its

---

inclusion not only of its essential portion, but also of the non-essential prayers and ceremonies added to give it further expressiveness. The context of the particular passage indicates which of these senses is the one there intended.

grace and power, which is chiefly the power of consecrating and offering the **true Body** and **Blood** of the **Lord** (Council of Trent, Sess. **XXIII.** *De Sacr. Ord.* Can. 1) in that sacrifice which is no nude commemoration of the sacrifice of the Cross' (*ibid.* Sess. XXII. *De Sacr. Miss.* Can. 3).

16. CATHOLIC DOCTRINE ON THE INTENTION OF THE MINISTER.

It has been said that besides a valid rite a proper *intention* on the part of the minister is required for the valid administration of a Sacrament. This proper intention is an 'intention to do what the Church does,' and it is necessary because the sacramental efficacy is attached, not to the words and ceremonies regarded physically as mere sounds and gestures, but to these as expressing the intentional purpose of one who has been appointed the minister of Christ and His Church, and desires to act in that capacity. And since intention is in itself an internal fact, and the further question arises how we are to judge whether the minister has it or not, the answer is that the Church must leave to the Providence of God all that does not disclose its character externally; but that, in so far as the minister does externally manifest the character of his intention, the Church is bound to deal with it. And her mode of dealing with it is as indicated by the Bull:

When anyone has rightly and seriously made use of the due form and the matter requisite for effecting or conferring the Sacrament he is considered by the very fact to do what the Church does. . . . On the other hand if the rite be changed, with the manifest intention of introducing another rite not approved by the Church, and of rejecting what the Church does, and what by the institution of Christ belongs to the nature of

D

the Sacrament, then it is clear that not only is the necessary intention wanting to the Sacrament, but that the intention is adverse to and destructive of the Sacrament.

17. STATEMENT OF DEFECTS IN ANGLICAN ORDINATIONS.

This exposition of its meaning has not travelled one whit beyond the brief language of the Bull, and that the doctrine stated is that universally taught by the Catholic Church may be seen from the writings of her theologians. Since, then, these are the principles by which she is wont to pronounce on the sufficiency of all disputed rites brought under her notice, she could not do otherwise than apply them to your own rites in the recent inquiry. The only question could be as to the fidelity of the application, and to this question, with the aid of your criticisms, we can now address ourselves.

The pronouncement of the Bull falls into three divisions. *First, the essential part* of the original Anglican rite, or what purports to be such, is examined to see if it contains words and ceremonies capable of bearing the definite signification required. *Secondly, the rite as a whole* is examined, in the light of the circumstances which governed its compilation, to see if it can be rationally taken as having been intended to express the conveyance of such a priesthood and episcopate as has been described. *Thirdly*, the Bull considers whether there are sufficient traces of the rite having been administered with the *intention* to do what the (Catholic) Church does. In each case the conclusion is adverse to your Orders.

18. THE INTENTION OF THE MINISTER DEFECTIVE.

As this last point is comparatively simple, we may clear the ground by saying now the little that needs to be said about it. A minister of the Anglican Church, unless there are external indications to the contrary, is presumed to *intend*, when he administers her rites, what she herself intends by them. Now, as we shall see, the Bull gathers, when dealing with the second of the above-stated points, that the Anglican rite for **Holy Orders**, which is obviously not an approved rite of the Catholic Church, was, on the contrary, set up in opposition to the Catholic rite, with the express object of rejecting that kind of priesthood for the conveyance of which the Catholic rite was instituted. The intention, therefore, of the Anglican clergy, coinciding with that of their own Church, is opposed to the intention of the Catholic Church, and so is ‘adverse to and destructive of the Sacrament.’

19. THE ESSENTIAL FORM DEFECTIVE.

Now about the *essential part* of the Anglican Ordination rite. Do the rites for the priesthood and the episcopate—for the Bull passes over the diaconate in the interests of brevity—contain words and ceremonies capable of *definitely signifying a true Catholic episcopate and presbyterate* or its grace and power? Both these rites have the ceremony of imposition of hands with an accompanying form of words, and it is natural to look here for the essential part of the rite. Are, then, these ceremonies and words sufficient?

20. THE FORM OF 1552 DOES NOT SIGNIFY DEFINITELY.

Whether imposition of hands is sufficient in the Western Church, or, as some theologians hold, a delivery of the sacrificial instruments is further required, the Bull does not decide. It was not necessary to decide that difficult question, since in the Anglican rite the *defect of form* is decisive,[1] as we are now to see. In the rite for the presbyterate, as it stood till 1662, the form was, *Receive the Holy Ghost,* and no one can say that these words of themselves signify the priesthood in any way, for they are quite indefinite. It is true that they were followed by the words, *Whose sins thou dost forgive they are forgiven; and whose sins thou dost retain they are retained: and be thou a faithful dispenser of the Word of God and of His Holy Sacraments: In the name of the Father* &c.; and by these others, whilst the Bible was delivered into the hands of the candidate, *Take thou authority to preach the Word of God and to minister the Holy Sacraments in this congregation, where thou shalt be appointed.* And it has been claimed that these further addresses to the candidates furnish the necessary determination of meaning, and should have been taken into account by the Bull. But to remit sins is not to offer sacrifice; nor, although the sacrifice is intimately connected with one of the Sacraments, do the words *Be thou a faithful dispenser . . . of His Holy Sacraments* draw special attention to that particular Sacrament, still less bring into prominence its sacrificial aspect. Nor does it avail to say that Our Lord used these words to confer the priesthood, and that therefore they must

---

[1] This, and not forgetfulness of its existence (see *Responsio*, Section VI.), is the reason why Leo XIII. makes no mention in his recent Bull of the *Instructio pro Armenis* of Eugenius IV. See Appendix II.

have been sufficient for the purpose. For it is not true that Our Lord conferred the priesthood by the use of these words. He had conferred the priesthood on His apostles at the Last Supper by the words, *Do this in remembrance of Me* (cp. *Council of Trent*, Sess. XXII. cap. ix. Can. 2). What He did on Easter evening by the words *Whose sins you shall forgive* was to annex to the priesthood the supplementary power of forgiving sins, or possibly only to indicate that it had been annexed already.

In like manner the form for the episcopate, as it stood till 1662, was wanting in the necessary signification. This form was, *Take the Holy Ghost, and remember that thou stir up the grace of God which is in thee by imposition of hands, for God hath not given us the spirit of fear, but of power, and love, and soberness.* And there followed (and follow) immediately, along with the delivery of the Bible, the words, '*Give heed unto reading, exhortation, and doctrine. Think upon these things contained in this book; be diligent in them, that the increase coming thereby may be manifest unto all men. Take heed unto thyself, and unto teaching, and be diligent in doing them: for by doing this thou shalt save thy soul, and them that hear thee. Be to the flock of Christ a shepherd, not a wolf; feed them, devour them not: hold up the weak, heal the sick, bind together the broken, bring again the outcasts, seek the lost. Be so merciful that you may not be too remiss: so minister discipline that you forget not mercy: that when the Chief Shepherd shall come, ye may receive the immarcessible crown of glory through Jesus Christ our Lord.* There is nothing here to express the episcopate or its special grace. The address to the candidate would be as suitable if made to one who was then receiving the priesthood. Nor are there solid grounds for supposing them to be the words, at all events the only words, by which St. Paul conferred the episcopate on St. Timothy. Nor when separated from their context in the epistle can they, without violence done to the usual laws of speech, be deemed to retain their reference to that disciple.

21. THE ADDITIONS IN 1662 USELESS.

Of course in 1662 a defining clause was added to each of these forms: (*Receive the Holy Ghost*) *for the office and work of a priest in the Church of God now committed unto thee by the imposition of our hands*, and (*Take the Holy Ghost*) *for the office and work of a Bishop in the Church of God now committed unto thee by the imposition of our hands, in the name of the Father* &c. The Bull takes note of these additions, which are undeniably an improvement, and might, apart from the further reason to be given presently, have furnished the necessary degree of definiteness. But whatever may have been the motive of these additions you will not disagree with Leo XIII. when he says that, not having been made till a century after your succession was started, they can have no bearing on the question of your Orders.

22. THE DEFICIENCY NOT SUPPLIED BY OTHER PRAYERS IN THE RITE.

Still it is urged by some on your side with whom you seem to agree (Section XV.) that there are at all events other prayers in your rite which clearly designate the office to be given; and that these can be treated as integral portions of your form, as it ran before 1662, and so supply for the deficiency imputed to the words

Receive the Holy Ghost &c. The Bull, however, anticipating somewhat the conclusion of a subsequent paragraph, very reasonably asks how any of these other prayers can be thought to designate the priesthood and episcopate in the Catholic sense, when it is notorious that this is just the meaning which the compilers were studious to exclude from the entire service.

Leo XIII. in rejecting this plea implies that, besides the reason given, another or others exist which would of themselves require its rejection. Of these one must certainly have been the moral disunion between these other prayers and the imposition of hands. The 'other prayer' which, so far as its text is concerned, is best adapted to supply the needed element of definiteness is the prayer, *Almighty God, Giver of all good things . . . behold these Thy servants now called to the office of priesthood* (or *episcopate*). But it is found in your present Ordinal far removed from the imposition of hands, being in fact the Collect for the day attached to the Communion Service. It is on this prayer, nevertheless, that your Graces fix, instructing us that before 1662 (it) 'was part of the form and used to be said by the Bishop immediately before the examination'; and that, 'if it has now been removed elsewhere,' this is because 'the new words' (added in 1662) 'clearly express the same sense' (Section XV.). But, even when said just before the examination of the candidates, this prayer was still considerably separated from the imposition of hands, as may be seen from your Prayer Book; and we cannot help thinking that your Graces in accepting this hypothesis had forgotten what you maintain elsewhere. For in Section XIX. you assure us that your Fathers when changing their Ordination rites 'aimed at simplicity and concentrated the parts of the whole rite as it were on one prominent point, so that no one could doubt at what moment the grace and power of the priesthood was given' (Section XIX.). Nor can we help thinking that on reflection you will perceive the incongruity of supposing that the ordaining Bishop was intended first to begin the words of actual ordination, then to interrupt them in order to ascertain at great length if the candidate were fit for the office, and afterwards to resume the interrupted ceremony in highly ambiguous language. Still, as you do press this hypothesis of a form consisting of two parts thus widely separated from each other, we can only reply that on no Catholic principles of judgment could words so widely separated, and with matter of so different a kind interjected between them, be considered as morally united.

The most, in short, that could be claimed for this or any other prayer or statement, whether in the body of your service or in its preface, is this, that, if only the expressions used had been meant in a Catholic sense, they would have served to define a true priesthood and episcopate as the graces intended to be conveyed by the use of the rite. This, however, would not have sufficed. The definite signification, as has already been explained, must be found in the *essential part*, in the matter and form morally united together. For otherwise that incongruity results which an eminent Roman Canonist in the *Revue Anglo-Romaine* (February 29, 1896) has, though with perhaps an excessive concession as regards the outlying parts of your rite, so graphically described:

> The compilers of the Ordinal ... have forgotten no preliminary. There is the presentation of the elect, and afterwards his oath. Next the Archbishop addresses the people in an Allocution suited to the occasion, and says the prayer over the candidate whilst the

singing and recitation of the Litanies proceeds. Then follows the prayer, *Almighty God, Giver of all good things*, of which I have spoken. Suddenly, just when the decisive moment has arrived, the Ordinal fails of its purpose. It has not a word to designate the office conferred. All the preparations for the marriage are made, the bride and bridegroom are at the foot of the altar. A moment ago they were expressing their mutual affection in a hundred eloquent fashions, and now when the instant has arrived for pronouncing the decisive word 'Yes,' they shut themselves up in a stubborn silence.

23. OBJECTION CONSIDERED: ANCIENT FORMS NOT DEFINITE; NATIONAL CHURCHES MAY COMPOSE THEIR OWN FORMS.

This is how the Bull reasons. But you have your reply. You tell us that we assume what you are not prepared to concede. You deny the necessity of a definite matter (Section IX.), or, at all events, of a definite form, and you inquire 'what authority the Pope has for discovering it' (Section XI.), suggesting that he has nothing better to support his contention than the authority of the schoolmen, 'who,' you say, 'were the first to teach that each of the Sacraments of the Church ought to have a single matter and form exactly defined.' You tell us likewise that we cut the ground from under our own feet when we claim that valid Ordinals always make mention of the sacrifice or of the high priesthood in the respective rites for the two Orders, alleging that many of the rites which the Holy See has tolerated are quite silent on the subject. And in this uncertainty of authoritative direction you claim for yourselves the 'liberty of National Churches to reform their own rites,' with one only proviso, that 'nothing is omitted which has been ordered by the Word of God, or the known and certain statutes of the Universal Church' (Section VIII.).

24. ANSWER—'NATIONAL' CHURCHES HAVE NO SUCH POWER.

These allegations constitute as it were your first line of defence, and we have not failed to notice them. But it is here particularly that you have misconceived the meaning of the Bull, and fallen into grave errors of fact. We readily allow that Holy Scripture has left us no adequate guidance on this point, but the Catholic Church has never supposed that Holy Scripture to the exclusion of Tradition is the sole rule of faith. As for the expression 'statutes of the Universal Church' we do not understand whether under it, or under the phrase 'Catholic Fathers,' which you employ in a similar passage (Section IX.), you desire to include the constant Tradition of the Catholic Church. But if it were true that our only sources of guidance have left us in such ignorance of the essentials of a valid Ordinal, surely the inference would be, not that National Churches (or, as we should prefer to call them, Local Churches) are at liberty to cut themselves loose from a constant Tradition, and unfettered by any other restrictions to devise Ordinals according to the requirements of their own local conceptions, but rather that they must not omit or reform anything in those forms which immemorial Tradition has bequeathed to us. For such an immemorial usage, whether or not it has in the course of ages incorporated superfluous accretions, must, in the estimation of those who believe in a divinely guarded, visible Church, at least have retained whatever is necessary; so that in adhering rigidly to the rite handed down to us we can always feel secure; whereas, if we omit or change anything, we may perhaps be abandoning just that element which is essential. And this sound method is that which the Catholic Church has always followed, as Morinus testifies in a well-known passage.

We deem it necessary for the reader to know that the modern Roman Pontifical contains all which was in the earlier Pontificals; but that the earlier Pontificals do not contain all that is in the modern Roman Pontifical. For various pious and religious reasons some things have been added to the recent Pontificals which are wanting in all the ancient editions. And the more recent any Pontificals are the more these [additions] obtrude themselves. . . . But this is a wonderful and impressive fact, that in all the volumes, ancient, more modern, and contemporary, there is ever one form of Ordination both as regards words and as regards ceremony, and *the later books omit nothing which was in the older.* Thus *the modern form of Ordination differs neither in word nor in ceremony from that used by the ancient Fathers*.[1]

Morinus is here speaking of the Roman Pontifical in its different editions, ancient and modern, and his words, therefore, include the Pontificals used in England by the pre-Reformation Church—for these, as you are aware, are but so many editions of the Roman Pontifical, with some slight variations, mostly additions, in palpably unessential points. What he says of the Western Pontificals might be said of the Eastern likewise—at all events, of those which are in use in the Uniat Churches, and indeed in all others, unless possibly in some outlying and neglectful community. As for the alleged right of local Churches to reform their rites freely, we are not aware in what quarter you have sought for illustrations of its exercise. That in earlier times local Churches were permitted to *add* new

---

[1] *De Sacris Ordinationibus*, pt. iii. p. 10. Morinus is here using the term 'form' in the first of the three senses distinguished in the footnote to page 31.

prayers and ceremonies is acknowledged, as the quotation from Morinus shows. But that they were also permitted to *subtract* prayers and ceremonies in previous use, and even to remodel the existing rites in the most drastic manner, is a proposition for which we know of no historical foundation, and which appears to us absolutely incredible. Hence Cranmer, in taking this unprecedented course, acted, in our opinion, with the most inconceivable rashness.

25. ANCIENT FORMS ALL DEFINITE AND IDENTICAL IN TYPE.

But you are also mistaken in thinking that matters have been left by Our Lord in so much uncertainty, and that there is no one definite form which has everywhere prevailed in the Catholic Church, both in the East and in the West. If, indeed, you mean merely that no *identical form of words* has always and everywhere been in use, but that, on the contrary, several different forms of words have been recognised by the Holy See as sufficient, you say what all will admit, and the Bull nowhere denies. Although, even as regards these various forms of words—the Roman, the Greek, the Maronite, the Nestorian, the Armenian, &c.—it should be observed that they are not numerous, not twelve, according to the most liberal estimate. Their origins too, being unrecorded, and belonging to the earliest Christian centuries, cannot be so confidently referred to an exercise of local liberty on the part of National Churches.

The Bull, however—when, passing over controversies about the *matter*, it lays down that the *form* of Holy Orders must be *definite*—is requiring, not that the form should always consist of the same words, but that it should always be conformed to *the same definite type.* Hence it goes on to say in what this definiteness of type is to consist. The form must, it says, always 'definitely express the sacred Order of the priesthood (or episcopate), *or* its grace and power, which is chiefly the power of consecrating and offering the Body and Blood of the Lord.'

26. A STRANGE MISCONCEPTION IN THE 'RESPONSIO.'

You will see now why we have characterised as misconception your contention that a definite form is essential in no Sacrament save Baptism, and, therefore, not in Holy Order. But we also notice another and somewhat surprising misconception in your further contention that the particular definite signification which the Pope deems essential to Holy Order is not discoverable in many of the forms which the Holy See, nevertheless, allows to be valid. You say that many of these forms are silent about the 'priesthood,' or 'high priesthood,' or 'the power to offer sacrifice'; and you give instances in support of your words. The rites to which you point are the very ancient form in the so-called Canons of St. Hippolytus, the form in the Leonine Sacramentary, a document of the sixth century or earlier, and the form in the Leofric Missal[1]—three forms, of which the first has been supposed by some writers to have been that used by the Roman Church in the third century; the second is the form still found

---

[1] The *Responsio* points also in another place (see the footnote to its Appendix on the Gordon case) to the alleged recognition by the Holy See, in 1704, of the sufficiency of the mere words *Accipe Spiritum Sanctum.* On this see Appendix III.

in the Roman Pontifical in all its various editions, though many other prayers are now added to it; the third is thought by many to belong to the old Gallican rite, long since disused, and now lost. These forms, however, fully satisfy the requirements of the Bull.

You have failed to observe the word 'or' in the proposition in which the Bull states what the requirements are. The proposition is disjunctive. The rite for the priesthood, the Pope says, 'must definitely express the sacred Order of the priesthood *or* its grace and power, which is chiefly the power of consecrating and offering the true Body and Blood of the Lord.' You do not seem to have perceived the importance of this little word 'or,' and have taken it to be the equivalent of 'and.' What Leo XIII. means is that the Order to which the candidate is being promoted must be distinctly indicated *either* by its accepted name *or* by an explicit reference to the grace and power which belongs to it. And, of course, he means us to understand that the same alternative requirements hold with regard to the form for the episcopate. The form must *either* designate the Order by its accepted name of 'bishop' *or* 'high priest,' *or* it must indicate that the high priesthood is the grace and power imparted. Nor is such a disjunctive statement unreasonable, for in the Catholic Church the alternative phrases are perfectly equivalent. The Catholic Church has always meant by the term 'priest' (*sacerdos*) a person appointed and empowered to offer sacrifice, and again by the terms 'priest' (*presbyter*) and 'bishop' (*episcopus*) or 'high priest' (*summus sacerdos*), the possessors of this power in its substance and in its plenitude respectively.

Had you not then mistaken this disjunctive for a conjunctive sentence you would, we think, have omitted the long disquisition of Sections XII. and XIII. of your Letter; for the true historical fact, a fact which was carefully investigated in the recent commissions, is that not one single Ordination rite which the Catholic Church has accepted is without one or other of these alternative modes of definite signification; and you can see that this is the case, even with the three forms which you have instanced, from Appendix IV. to this Letter, which gives the essential portions of all the forms which the Church has, or may have, at any time or in any way sanctioned.

27. A FURTHER OBJECTION CONSIDERED: DO THE TERMS 'BISHOP,' 'PRIEST,' OF THEMSELVES SIGNIFY DEFINITELY?

Before we leave this branch of the subject, one word may be useful to meet an objection which perhaps occurs to you. The terms 'priest,' 'bishop,' it may be said, are now declared to be the accepted terms to denote those who have received in substance or in plenitude the sacrificial power. Why, then, have they been rejected in an earlier part of this Letter as not bearing that meaning when they occur in your prayer, *Almighty God, Giver of all good things*? The objection is specious, but it forgets that words take their meanings from the communities in which they are used. Now in the Catholic Church the terms 'priest' and 'bishop' have always had a sacrificial meaning; and hence when used in our 'essential forms' they definitely convey the required sacrificial meaning. The same is true of the Oriental Communions which use these various ancient ordination forms—as may be seen, if anyone doubts the fact, by an inspection of their Liturgies for the Mass. But with your Communion it is dif-

ferent. Your Reformers no doubt retained the terms
'priest' and 'bishop' as the distinctive names of the
two higher degrees of their clergy—probably because
they did not dare to discard terms so long established
and so familiar. But whilst retaining the terms they
protested against the meanings attached to them by the
Catholics, and, insisting on the etymological signification, used them, and desired that in future they should
be used, to denote, not ministers empowered to offer
sacrifice, but pastors set over their flocks, to teach them,
to administer to them such Sacraments as they believed
in, and generally to tend them spiritually. This
meaning they professed to regard as that of Scripture
and of the Primitive Church, which explains the language
of the Preface of your Ordinal.

In illustration of this mode of employing the terms
we cannot do better than remind you of the well-known
passage from Hooker :

> Seeing, then, that sacrifice is now no part of the Church
> ministry, how should the name of priesthood be thereunto rightly
> applied? . . . The Fathers of the Church [this is Hooker's
> view] . . . call usually the ministry of the Gospel priesthood in
> regard of that which the Gospel hath proportionable to ancient
> sacrifices, namely, the communion of the Blessed Body and Blood
> of Christ, although it have properly now no sacrifice. As for
> the people, when they hear the name it draweth no more their
> minds to any cogitation of sacrifice than the name of a senator
> or an alderman causeth them to think on old age.[1]

Thus the mere employment of the terms 'priest'
and 'bishop' in one or two prayers in your rite would
go for nothing, even if in other respects those prayers,
or any of them, fulfilled the requirements of an essential
form. It has been shown, however, that they fail also

---

[1] *Eccles. Polity*, Bk. V. chap. lxxviii. § 3.

in these other respects, being separated from the imposition of hands. It is only *ex abundantia*, therefore, that your appeal to the use of these terms in the said prayers can be entertained by us at all.

28. DEFECT IN THE GENERAL CHARACTER OF THE ANGLICAN RITE.

It is a fact, then, that by employing rites from the 'essential forms' of which all definite signification of the grace and power of the priesthood are wanting, not even the traditional names of the Orders being there retained, your Ordinal has deprived itself of elements found in every Ordinal which the Catholic Church has ever recognised, and essential to the fundamental type of a sacramental form. On this ground alone its rejection was justified. Still the Bull has not stopped here. Leo XIII. has likewise viewed your rite from the standpoint which you yourselves suggest, for he has considered it *as a whole*, quite apart from the shortcomings of the 'essential forms' or words attached to the imposition of hands; and, judging it in the light of its own text and of the intentions of those who introduced it, he has asked himself whether even so it can be deemed to signify definitely the sacred Orders of the priesthood and episcopate as the Catholic Church understands them.

29. THE ANGLICAN RITE AS A WHOLE DOES NOT SIGNIFY THE CONVEYANCE OF A TRUE PRIESTHOOD.

The result has been only to confirm the judgment passed on the 'essential form' by showing how radically incompatible is your entire Ordinal with the

Catholic idea of the *sacerdotium*. Leo XIII. announces his judgment on this point in the following terms:

> For the full and accurate understanding of the Anglican Ordinal, besides what we have noted as to some of its parts, there is nothing more pertinent than to consider carefully the circumstances under which it was composed and publicly authorised. It would be tedious to enter into details, nor is it necessary to do so, as the history of that time is sufficiently eloquent as to the animus of the authors of the Ordinal against the Catholic Church, as to the abettors whom they associated with themselves from the heterodox sects, and as to the end they had in view. Being fully cognisant of the necessary connection between faith and worship, 'the law of believing and the law of praying,' under a pretext of returning to the primitive form, they corrupted the liturgical order in many ways to suit the errors of the Reformers. For this reason in the whole Ordinal not only is there no clear mention of the sacrifice, of consecration, of the *sacerdotium*, and of the power of consecrating and offering sacrifice, but, as we have just stated, every trace of these things, which had been in such prayers of the Catholic rite as they had not entirely rejected, was deliberately removed and struck out. In this way the native character—or spirit as it is called—of the Ordinal clearly manifests itself. Hence, if vitiated in its origin it was wholly insufficient to confer Orders then, it was impossible that in the course of time it should become sufficient.

Leo XIII. has here assumed, as he well might, that no entering into details was necessary to vindicate a statement in such conspicuous correspondence with the facts. You do, however, dispute the statement, which you call 'harsh and inconsiderate words' (Section XVI.), and you devote several sections to its refutation. From the contents indeed of these sections (Sections XVI.-XIX.) it appears that your objection is not so much to the account itself of what was discarded by your 'Fathers,' or of their beliefs and intentions, but rather to the implication that what they discarded was essential to a valid Ordinal, and that their object in discarding it was to disavow Catholic doctrines, and not, as you contend, to render the rites simpler. Still, as you do demur to the Pope's statement, it becomes necessary to call your attention to the new character imparted to your Ordinal by its makers, and to give some illustrations of what they believed and felt.

30. OMISSIONS AND CHANGES IN THE ORDINAL.

First as to the omissions and changes which characterise your Ordinal by comparison with the Ordinal which it superseded. The Pope says that he cannot find in it any trace of the sacrifice or of the *sacerdotium*, or of consecration, and is he not right? He means, of course, by 'consecration,' not the mere recitation of the words of institution with the belief that they bestow some kind of benediction on the bread and wine, but their recitation in the belief that they make the Body and Blood of Christ really and objectively present; just as he means by *sacerdotium* (a word left untranslated in the English version to obviate misconstruction) a sacrificial priesthood, and by 'sacrifice' a sacrifice in which Our Lord's Body and Blood is the thing offered. Can anyone discover traces of these in the Ordinal? With the terms of the form joined to the imposition of hands we have already dealt, and also with the use of the word 'priest' in some of your prayers and addresses, and likewise in the Preface; and we have shown that nothing can be inferred from these. Yet where else can any intimation be found that the graces imparted have reference to the consecration and oblation of the Body and Blood of Christ?

Nowhere of course; but your contention seems to be

that we must not argue *ex silentio*. It would be sufficient answer to this plea to point out that, at least according to the principles by which the Holy See must judge, an Ordination rite must *contain*, either explicitly or at least implicitly, the definite signification of what is essential to the Order conferred. But the silence of your Ordinal is not merely neutral; it speaks volumes. Look at the long address to the candidates at the beginning of the rite for the priesthood, and look at the series of questions which follow it. The very scope of these parts is to instruct the candidates in the nature and duties of their new office, and to ascertain publicly if their views concerning them are satisfactory. And yet throughout there is not one word of reference to the powers of consecration or sacrifice, whilst, on the other hand, the functions to which the candidates are called are becomingly described in language which exactly accords with the notion of a Protestant pastorate. In the rite for the episcopate the long address is wanting, but there is a similar series of questions and answers, to which the same criticism applies. Why was there such striking suppression unless it were that the makers of this Ordinal could find no place in their conception of the ministry for elements which in a Catholic ministry are essential? Next look at the Catholic Ordinal which was superseded. We are not now referring to the Catholic rite in its older and simpler style, such as we find it in the Leonine Sacramentary. Even there, indeed, the sacrificial character of the power communicated is not obscurely indicated, quite apart from the use of the sacrificial terms 'priest' and 'bishop.' But we are calling attention to this Catholic rite, as it was prescribed and employed, in England and on the Continent, at the time of the so-called Reformation.

It is this which Cranmer and his colleagues took in hand, and 'reformed.' It is with this, therefore, that their revised rite must be compared if we desire to interpret on rational principles the meaning of the latter. Now, that the Catholic rite in its mediæval stage abounded in words and ceremonies giving expression to the sacrificial character of the power to be conveyed, is so well known that we do not need to prove it. We will content ourselves therefore with recalling to mind the delivery of the sacrificial instruments, the clothing in the sacrificial vestments, the anointing of the hands, together with the addresses to the candidates accompanying these manual ceremonies. What we desire to accentuate is that these striking assertions of the sacrificial priesthood, which at the time were in almost immemorial possession, were all struck out of the Edwardine Ordinal.

Why was this? It could not have been, as you seem to suggest, because the Reformers wished to go back to what was primitive, for they cut out with an unsparing hand the most ancient as well as the most modern portions of the Catholic rite. It could not have been because, as you suggest again, they wished for a rite of great simplicity, for they could easily have retained some short sentence, such as '*sacerdotem oportet offerre, benedicere, præesse, prædicare, conficere et baptizare*'; or they could have constructed another short sentence of equivalent meaning. It could not have been for no reason at all. In short, the only and the sufficient reason for the suppression is that they disliked the notion of a sacrificing priesthood, which they alleged to be without warrant in Scripture, and desired to dissociate their Ordinal from all connection with it.

31. OMISSIONS AND CHANGES IN THE COMMUNION SERVICE.

This argument is strengthened when from the Ordinal itself we turn to your Communion Service. To put the matter briefly, if the First Prayer Book of Edward VI. is compared with the Missal, sixteen omissions can be detected of which the evident purpose was to eliminate the idea of sacrifice. Moreover, whereas even after that drastic treatment there still remained a few phrases and rubrics on which Gardiner could fasten, endeavouring to understand them as still asserting the Real Objective Presence and the True Sacrifice, all these phrases and rubrics were altered in the revised Prayer Book of 1552. Again, therefore, we must put the question: Why these systematic changes and suppressions, unless it were that your 'Fathers' wished to prevent their rites from continuing to express that 'grace and power which is chiefly the power of consecrating and offering the Body and Blood of the Lord'?

32. WHAT DID THE AUTHORS OF THE ORDINAL INTEND?

If the Pope was justified in saying that the Ordinal by its omissions and suppressions tells its own tale, is he not equally justified in what he has said about its authors and their beliefs and intentions? Is it not true that their very object in drawing up the new rite and substituting it for the old was to remove the sacrificial and sacerdotalist elements which were such a characteristic feature in the old rite? And if so, must not the true key to solve disputes about the meaning and effect of the new rite in any of its parts be sought precisely in the strongly expressed views of its authors?

33. WHO WERE THE AUTHORS OF THE ORDINAL?

But who were the authors of your Ordinal and the Prayer Book (for in this connection it is necessary to consider the two formularies together)? We put the question because it is well known that there were two parties among the prelates and divines concerned with the remodelling of your rites, and it has been claimed that these rites may not be interpreted by the views of one party rather than of the other.

Such a plea, however, even if it could be sustained, would be futile. If, indeed, the question were as to the lawfulness for a member of your Communion of determining for himself whether he would interpret your Ordinal as expressing the views of Cranmer or those of Gardiner, then there might be some advantage to such a person in raising it; for if he could make good his contention he would have secured for himself a measure of that liberty of private judgment which in your Communion is so much appreciated. But the question really raised is as to whether the language of your Ordinal *definitely* signifies the Orders of the priesthood or episcopate, or the respective graces and powers of each, such a definite signification being essential to its recognition by the Holy See as a valid rite. Now to claim that this Ordinal can be interpreted with equal justice and propriety as expressing the opinions of Cranmer on the nature of the ministry, and those of Gardiner, is nothing less than to allow that the rite, so far from being definite in its meaning, is indefinite and ambiguous, and that with an ambiguity extending so far as to cover both the assertion and the denial of the true Priesthood such as our Lord instituted. Clearly, then, to advance a plea like this is to acknowledge at once the justice of the Papal decision.

We do not, however, wish to claim support for the Papal decision by this means, because we feel that this strange plea for a twofold interpretation of your Ordinal cannot be sustained. Surely those who think that it can be sustained have not studied very carefully the facts. Archbishop Cranmer was the highest ecclesiastical authority at the time, and was likewise the leading spirit of the revisional movement. As for the other Bishops and divines engaged, the majority were Cranmer's supporters, in full agreement with his views and designs. In the Commission appointed to draw up the First Prayer Book, which, however, had been already prepared by Cranmer himself, five only out of the thirteen Commissioners belonged to the more Catholic-minded party. On the preparation of the Second Prayer Book and of the Ordinal in both its forms, this party seems to have had still less influence. In fact, what Cranmer's opponents did throughout was to offer an unsuccessful resistance at every stage. Thus, in the House of Lords, where each party could muster in its strength, the Bishops opposed to Cranmer were in a minority, not merely of the whole House, but even of their own Order, Cranmer's more attached supporters being reinforced by a few Opportunists.

If this minority consistently voted against the proposed formularies it was obviously because they found in them the expression, not of their own beliefs, but of the beliefs they disliked. How unnatural, then, to wish to interpret the said formularies by the views of the defeated minority instead of by the views of the triumphant majority! How unnatural, that is, to wish to interpret them as expressing the views which the minority held to be true, since to interpret them as the minority understood them is to interpret them by the views of the majority! For, to put it briefly, both parties were agreed that the rites meant what the majority believed, the majority on this account desiring their authorisation, and the minority their rejection. Gardiner, indeed, who was in prison throughout the entire period of the proceedings, caught, as has been already said, at a few phrases in the First Prayer Book when it was taken to him for signature, and persuaded himself that they could bear a Catholic meaning. But these few phrases were quickly changed in the Second Prayer Book into phrases about the genuine Protestantism of which he could no longer be mistaken. Perhaps we ought to add here that in censuring this fallacious principle of interpretation we are not suggesting that your Graces hold it. It is not advanced in your Letter, but it is usually advanced by the High Church party in your Communion, in whose hands it has become the principal instrument for affixing a more Catholic meaning to your rites. It is on this account that it has seemed opportune to consider it.

34. CRANMER'S DOCTRINE ON THE REAL PRESENCE.

When once it is realised that the true key to the meaning of the omissions and dubious phraseology of the Prayer Book and Ordinal is to be sought in the views and aims of Cranmer and his party, it becomes indisputable what the key is. The difficulty is indeed not to find but to select testimonies for citation, and it may even seem **superfluous to** cite testimonies at all in proof of so patent a fact. Still, we have promised some specimens, and will proceed now to give them. That you may understand better, however, the significance we attach to them, may we remind you again of what has been said above concerning the intimate connection between the doctrines of the Real Objective Presence, the Sacrifice, and the Priesthood? Without the Real Objective Presence there can be no true Sacrifice, and without a true Sacrifice no true Priesthood.

Cranmer wrote a long treatise entitled *A Defence of* **the** *True* **and** *Catholic Doctrine concerning the Sacrament of the Body* **and** *Blood of Christ*, and in the Preface he tells us very distinctly what were the principal ' corruptions ' he desired to see abolished :

What availeth it to take away beads, pardons, pilgrimages, **and such** other like Popery, so long **as** two chief roots remain unpulled up? Whereof so long as they remain will spring **again all** former impediments of the Lord's harvest and corruption of **His flock. The** rest is but branches and leaves . . . but the very body of the tree, or rather the roots of the weeds, is the Popish doctrine **of** transubstantiation, **of** the Real Presence of Christ's Flesh **and** Blood in **the** Sacrament of the Altar (as they call it), and **of** the Sacrifice **and** Oblation of Christ made by the priest for the salvation of the quick and the dead. Which roots, if they be suffered in the Lord's vineyard, they will overspread all the ground **again with the old** errors and superstitions.

Here we find the two doctrines which underlie **and** condition the doctrine **of a** true Priesthood formally declared to be the roots of evil which most of all needed destroying. This passage is really decisive as to Cranmer's rejection of the Catholic doctrine, but it will be satisfactory to know more precisely what he himself held; and, faithful to the engagement we have made, we will pass over what he says of transubstantiation. We have to do only with his opinions on the Real Presence.

He tells us that Christ is present in the bread and wine only figuratively:

> He is not in the bread spiritually (as He is in the man), nor in the bread corporally (as He is in heaven), but sacramentally only (as a thing is said to be in the figure by which it is signified).[1]

Hence it is true to say that He is not in the bread and wine at all, but only in the heart of the receiver:

> They teach that Christ is in the bread and wine; we (as the truth itself requires) teach that Christ is in those who worthily partake of the bread and wine. . . . They teach that Christ remains in the sacramental bread, even if it be kept a whole year; but that after the Sacrament has been received, when the bread is ground in the mouth and changed in the stomach, He departs to heaven; but we teach that Christ remains in the man who receives the bread worthily *as long as the man remains a member of Christ*.[2]

And this, he says in another place, is what is meant by a phrase in the First Prayer Book, afterwards removed as susceptible of a 'Popish' meaning:

> Therefore in the Book of the Holy Communion we do not pray absolutely that the bread and wine may be made the Body and Blood of Christ, but that *unto us* in that holy mystery they may be so; that is to say, that we may so worthily receive the same that we may be partakers of Christ's Body and Blood, and that therewith in spirit and in truth we may be spiritually nourished.[3]

It should be noticed, too, that it is only the worthy receiver of the Sacrament in whom Christ, according to Cranmer, is present.

---

[1] P. 238, Parker Society's edition.   [2] *Ibid.* pp. 52, 58.   [3] *Ibid.* p. 79.

Now mine intent and purpose in the fourth book is not to prove that evil men receive not the Body and Blood in the Sacrament (*although that be true*), but my chief purpose is to prove that evil men eat not Christ's Flesh, nor drink His Blood neither in the Sacrament nor out of the Sacrament; as on the other side good men eat and drink them *both in the Sacrament and out of the Sacrament*.[1]

And the reason is that 'they [the Body and Blood of Christ] cannot be eaten and drunken but by spirit and faith whereof ungodly men be destitute.'[2] What the nature of this faith is he teaches us in the same passage:

It is very necessary to know that Christ's Body cannot be eaten but spiritually by believing and remembering Christ's benefits, and revolving them in our mind, believing that as the bread and wine feed and nourish our bodies, so Christ feedeth and nourisheth our souls.[3]

In other words, this faith, by which alone the Body and Blood of Our Lord are truly received, is not faith as Catholics understand the term, but that illusory feeling of assurance which is called 'justifying faith' by the Lutherans and Calvinists; for it is described as a faith which the ungodly are incapable of having.

Clearly this doctrine is not the doctrine of a Real Objective Presence, for that Presence is a presence quite as much in the unworthy and unbelieving as in the worthy. The attitude, indeed, of the two classes of communicants towards it is different, and so too are its effects upon their souls. But the Presence itself is the same in both. It is the same again on the altar, as in the hearts of men, and ought in consequence to be adored there just as it is adored in heaven, a point which Cranmer understood very well, for he had the logic of his convictions. Disbelieving in any Real

---

[1] *A Defence*, &c., p. 203. [2] *Ibid.* [3] *Ibid.* p. 204.

Presence of Our Lord in the Sacrament, he denounced the worship of the Blessed Sacrament as idolatry. Indeed, this was his great complaint against the Catholic doctrine, that it led to idolatry:

And yet have the very antichrists (the subtlest enemies that Christ hath) by their fine inventions and crafty scholastic divinity deluded many simple souls and brought them to this horrible idolatry, to worship things visible and made with their own hands . . . [and although they say] that they worship not the Sacraments which they see with their eyes, but that thing which they believe to be really and corporally in the Sacraments, yet why do they run from place to place to gaze at the things which they see if they worship them not, giving thereby occasion to them that be ignorant to worship that which they see?[1]

35. CRANMER'S DOCTRINE ON THE SACRIFICE OF THE MASS.

So much to illustrate his denial of the Real Objective Presence, the doctrine without which the Catholic doctrine of the Sacrifice cannot subsist. That his hostility to the doctrine of the True Sacrifice was equally pronounced will appear sufficiently from the following passage:

All such priests as pretend to be Christ's successors in making a sacrifice of Him, they be His most heinous and horrible adversaries. For never no person made a sacrifice of Christ, but He Himself only. . . . For what needeth any more sacrifices if Christ's sacrifice be perfect and sufficient? . . . Wherefore all Popish priests that presume to make every day a sacrifice of Christ either must they make Christ's sacrifice vain, unperfect, and unsufficient, or else is their sacrifice in vain which is added to the sacrifice, which is already of itself sufficient and perfect.[2]

And that the object of this denunciation was not a popular error current in some quarters, but the

---

[1] *A Defence*, &c., pp. 228, 229.   [2] *Ibid.* p. 348.

recognised doctrine of the Catholic Church, is manifest from the way in which he continues :

> But it is a wondrous thing to see what shifts and cautels the **Popish antichrists devise** to colour and cloke their wicked errors. . . . **For the** Papists, to excuse themselves, do say that they make **no** new sacrifice, nor none other sacrifice than Christ made (for they be not so blind but they see **that then** they should add another sacrifice **to** Christ's sacrifice, and so make His sacrifice unperfect); but **they** say that they make the selfsame sacrifice for sin that Christ made Himself. And here they run headlong into the **foulest and** most heinous **error** that ever **was imagined.**

36. CRANMER'S DOCTRINE ON THE CHRISTIAN PRIESTHOOD.

From passages like these, which occur in great abundance, we see that there was no place in Cranmer's system for any doctrine which could recognise in the Christian ministry a power of consecrating and offering the Body of Christ, and could require an Ordinal suited to convey it. He would have been flagrantly inconsistent with himself had he conceived otherwise of the Christian minister than as one possessing only the same powers as the layman, but placed over the people in the interests of public order, to rule them, to instruct them, and to lead their devotions. And this is what he teaches in the following passage :

> Christ made no **such** difference between the priest and the layman that the priest should make oblation and sacrifice for the layman, **and eat the** Lord's Supper for him all alone, and distribute and apply it as him liketh. Christ made **no such** difference, **but the** difference that is **between** the priest and the layman **in** this matter is only in **the** ministration. . . . As in a prince's house the officers and ministers prepare the table, and yet other, as well **as they,** eat the meat and drink the drink,

so do the priests and ministers prepare the Lord's Supper, read the Gospel, and rehearse Christ's words, but all the people say thereto, Amen. All remember Christ's death, all give thanks to God, all repent and offer themselves an oblation to Christ, all take Him for their Lord and Saviour, and spiritually feed upon Him; and in token thereof they eat the bread and drink the wine in His mystical Supper.[1]

There is, too, Cranmer's well-known answer to Henry VIII.'s question in 1540.

The ministers of God's word under his Majesty be the Bishops, Parsons, Vicars, and such other priests as be appointed by His Highness to that ministration: as, for example, the Bishop of Canterbury, the Bishop of Duresme, the Bishop of Winchester, the Parson of Winwick &c. All the said officers and ministers be appointed, assigned, and elected, and in every place, by the laws and orders of the Kings and Princes. In the admission of many of these officers be divers comely ceremonies and solemnities used, which be not of necessity, but only for a good order and seemly fashion; for if such offices and ministrations were committed without such solemnity, they were nevertheless truly committed. And there is no more promise of God that grace is given in the committing of the ecclesiastical office, than it is in the committing of the civil office.[2]

Clearly an answer which is in such logical consistency with the rest of his system gave not the impression of the moment, but his deliberately thought-out opinion.

37. THE DOCTRINES OF CRANMER'S COLLEAGUES.

Such were Cranmer's own beliefs, and it is easy to support them by similar illustrations from the writings of Ridley, his chief lieutenant in the work of so-called

---
[1] *A Defence*, &c., p. 350.
[2] *Stillingfleet MSS.* XXI. i.; Lambeth, 1108, fol. 71.

reform; and likewise, though less copiously (for they wrote less), from the language used by other members of his party. All speak in the same tone. Some specimens of these utterances of Cranmer's colleagues may be seen in the Appendix (V.); but here, in the text, we may be content to appeal to the loud-tongued denunciations of the Mass and massing priests heard on every side at that time, to the systematic destruction of altars throughout the land, and to the teaching of the Articles.

38. THE DESTRUCTION OF ALTARS.

The destruction of the altars was a measure so distinct in its meaning that we have never been able to conceive how that meaning could be misunderstood. The measure meant a bitter hatred of the Mass, and a hatred directed against the Mass itself, not merely against some obscure abuse such as recent writers have sought in vain to unearth from the ambiguous phrases of one or two theological writers. *Usum non tollit abusus.* Surely if these reformers had desired only to remove an abuse, but were full of reverence for the great Christian Sacrifice itself, they would not have destroyed and desecrated the altars, and substituted tables in their place, alleging as their reason, in unqualified terms, that ' the form of a table shall more move the simple from the superstitious opinions of the Popish Mass unto the right use of the Lord's Supper. For the use of an altar is to make sacrifice upon it; the use of a table is to serve men to eat upon it.' [1]

---

[1] Ridley's *Works*, Parker Society's edition, p. 322. See also Dom Gasquet's *Edward VI. and Book of Common Prayer*, p. 266.

39. THE DOCTRINE OF ARTICLES XXVIII. AND XXIX.

The interpretation of the Articles seems in these days to be delivered over to the caprices of unchecked private judgment and inclination. If, however, they be rationally dealt with, they yield a sense which is at least plain and intelligible, and (to speak only of those bearing on our subject) in harmony with the doctrinal system we have gathered from Cranmer's writings. Thus in Article XXVIII., as it left Cranmer's hands, the mode of eating is declared to be an exercise of faith. The Article says, indeed, 'with faith'; but the evident sense is that faith is the means whereby the Body and Blood of Christ is received, for to those who eat thus 'with faith,' 'the bread' (the *bread*, not the *Body of Christ*) is said to be the 'communication of Christ's Body,' the implication being that to those who do not eat with faith Christ's Body is not communicated. Moreover, it is stated in so many words in the clause added in 1563, that 'the *mean* whereby the Body of Christ is received and eaten is faith.' Transubstantiation meets with an unqualified denunciation, which is enclosed between the clause declaring that the eating is the same as believing, and a clause denying the possibility of a 'Real and Bodily Presence, as they' (*i.e.* the 'Papists') 'term it, in the Sacrament of the Lord's Supper.' Finally there is a declaration against the adoration of the Blessed Sacrament in its various forms of expression: 'The Sacrament of the Lord's Supper was not commanded by Christ's ordinance to be kept, carried about, lifted up, nor worshipped.' In 1562 the paragraph about the Real Presence was taken out, probably in deference to the wishes of some who at that time held Ubiquitarian **views about** the Sacred Humanity; but another Article was inserted—now Article XXIX.—declaring **in** its **title** in **the** most direct terms that the 'wicked . . . do not eat the Body **of** Christ in the use of the Supper.'[1]

[1] We are aware of the efforts **that** have been made to give **to** these **two** Articles (XXVIII. and XXIX.) an interpretation consonant with belief in the Real Objective Presence. It has been urged (Forbes on the *Thirty-nine Articles, in loc.*), that in Article XXVIII. the Body of Christ is said to be 'given, taken, and **eaten**,' and stress has been laid on this triplet of terms. '**Taking**' **and** '**eating**,' **it** is said, being distinct words, must be meant to **denote distinct** actions, of which, since one, the 'eating,' **is** through the exercise of **faith, the** other, 'taking,' must **denote** an external **act, and, being coupled** with its correlative 'giving,' **be** understood to declare an objective 'taking' of something objectively 'given,' which can be nothing else than the true Body and Blood of Christ present on the altar. It has been also contended (by Dr. Pusey in the *Eirenicon*), as regards Article XXIX., that the phrase to 'partake of Christ' by general agreement denotes a beneficial eating of the **sacramental** food, so that it is quite consonant with Catholic doctrine to **deny, as** the Article does, such eating to the wicked.

These ingenious interpretations of phrases which in their obvious sense are calculated to convey quite an opposite sense are too subtle to impress many minds. They do not, however, touch the argument advanced in the text. That interpretation of a formulary is to be preferred which, whilst fitting its words, accords with the otherwise well known and clearly expressed opinion of its authors and their sympathisers, and it is pointed out in the text that the words of the two Articles, XXVIII. and XXIX., correspond exactly with the **doctrine of Cranmer.**

Thus Cranmer, as the quotations **from his writings** given **above** bear witness, places the difference between the Catholics and his own party in this, that the Catholics teach that ' Christ is in the bread and wine,' but **he** and his friends that ' Christ is in those who worthily partake of the bread and wine; ' and Article XXVIII. similarly says that to those who ' rightly, worthily, and with faith receive the same, the bread is a communion of the Body of Christ,' whilst the following Article (added later, and presumably for greater clearness) denies absolutely that the wicked eat or drink more than the sign or sacrament of the Body and Blood of Christ — in other words, than **the mere bread** and wine. Moreover, Article XXVIII., in the form which Cranmer **gave** it, denies expressly that the Body of Christ can be anywhere else **save in** heaven.

Cranmer again says that Christ's body cannot be eaten but '*spiritually*,' which he explains to be ' by *believing* and remembering Christ's benefits,' in other words, ' by an act of faith; ' and Article XXVIII. similarly says that it ' is given, taken, and eaten only after an heavenly and *spiritual*

Article XXXI. pronounces on the **Mass.** It first describes it by a definition which every Catholic would accept, 'the Sacrifices of Masses, in the which it was commonly said that the priest did offer Christ for the quick and the dead,' and then denounces it—it, so described—as incompatible with the offering of Christ once made on the Cross. And Article **XXXV.** calls the doctrine of the Homilies 'godly and wholesome,' whereas Homily **XV.** of Book II. bids us ' take heed lest of the memory of the Lord's supper be made a sacrifice,' and says we 'need no sacrificing priest, no Mass.'

40. CRANMER'S **METAPHORICAL USE OF THE TERM 'REAL PRESENCE.'**

Whilst, however, Cranmer and his fellow-reformers denounced in unmeasured language the doctrines of the Real Presence, the Sacrifice, and the Priesthood, as the Catholic Church understands them, it must be acknowledged that at times, though in an evidently half-hearted manner, the self-same men are found claiming each of these three terms as expressing a portion of

manner,' and that 'the mean whereby' it is received and eaten in the Supper is *faith*.

Cranmer, once more, deduces from this doctrinal statement the inappropriateness of worshipping the Host; and the Article similarly denounces this practice in its different forms as contrary to the institution of Christ.

With a correspondence so complete in all the salient points, how can it be rational to interpret Cranmer in one way and the formulary in another? It is true that these Articles in their present form are due partly to Cranmer and partly to the Elizabethan revisers, and among the latter to Bishop Guest. But this only proves that the authors and revisers of the Articles were in substantial doctrinal agreement; and as for Bishop Guest, the penman of the Elizabethan revision of Article XXVIII., when it is claimed for him that he was personally a believer in the Real Objective Presence, and must have intended to express what he believed, the extracts from his works in Appendix VI. show that the sense in which he held this doctrine was very different from that of the Catholic Church.

their belief. **It is** important that the true character of this inconsistency should be understood, for it is through the failure to understand it that men who were the most bitter in their invectives against **the** Mass are occasionally cited as having been among its defenders. The explanation is, however, very simple. The 'Reformers' had no love for terms which, understood in **their** *prima facie* sense, affirmed the very doctrines they **were** rejecting. But they were in this dilemma. They **were** confronted **by** their opponents with the writings of the Fathers in which these terms constantly occur. They were constrained, **therefore, to do one or other of** two things: **to** confess that the Primitive Church no less than **the** Church of their own **days was** against them; or else to claim that the language of the Fathers suitably expressed the '**Reformed**' doctrine, and endeavour to make good the claim by retaining the old terms but altering their sense. As the former of these two courses would **have** been fatal to their position, Cranmer and his friends naturally preferred the latter, and their writings are full of illustrations of the dexterity with which they could quibble over the meaning of the well-known **terms—Real** Presence, Sacrifice, and Priesthood.

Thus, to confine ourselves to Cranmer, we may take note of such **a** typical passage as the following, **in which he** claims to hold the Real Presence:

As for the real presence of Christ in the Sacrament, I grant that He is really present after such sort as you [Gardiner] expound 'really.'[1]

The statement sounds most satisfactory; but he continues, 'that is **to say,** in deed and yet but spiritually.'

[1] *A Defence, &c.*, p. **127.**

Even so, his words can bear a Catholic sense, and he is able to add with truth: 'For you [*i.e.* Gardiner, and with him all Catholic theologians] say yourself that He is but after a spiritual manner there, and so is He spiritually honoured, as St. Augustine saith.' There is, however, a very subtle equivocation latent under this assimilation of terminology. Catholic theologians, when they speak in this manner, are contrasting 'spiritual' with 'carnal,' and mean, as has been explained already, that in the Blessed Sacrament Our Lord's Body, though still a body, exists after the manner of a spirit (cp. 1 Cor. xv. 44). Cranmer, on the other hand, meant by the term 'spiritually present' that Our Lord's Body, though itself in heaven, is able, by its innate power, to produce certain spiritual effects in the soul on earth which believes. He tells us this himself in some of the passages already quoted, and he tells it still more categorically in the preface to the treatise *On the Lord's Supper*, from which the above well-sounding words are taken.

When I say, and repeat many times in my book, that the Body of Christ is present in them that worthily receive the Sacrament; lest any man should mistake my words, and think that I mean that, although Christ be not corporally in the outward visible signs, yet He is corporally in the persons that duly receive them, this is to advertise the reader that I mean no such thing; but my meaning is *that the force, the grace, the virtue and benefit* of Christ's Body that was crucified for us, and of His Blood that was shed for us, *be really and effectually present* with all them that duly receive the Sacraments. But all this I understand of His *spiritual* presence, of the which He saith, 'I will be with you until the world's end,' and 'wheresoever two or three be gathered together in My name, there am I in the midst of them,' and 'he that eateth My Flesh and drinketh My Blood dwelleth in Me and I in him.' Nor no more truly is He corporally or really present in the due ministration of the Lord's Supper, than he is in the due ministration of baptism:

that is to say, *in both spiritually by grace*. And *wheresoever* in the Scripture *it is said that Christ, God, or the Holy Ghost is in any man, the same is understood spiritually by grace.*

Nothing could be more decisive than this. Being present spiritually, he tells us, is being present by grace; and being present by grace means that the grace, not the Body, of Our Lord is *really* present in the soul. This is what we Catholics should ourselves say of the presence of Our Lord with those gathered together in His name, or in those undergoing Baptism. But a Presence in the Holy Eucharist which is the same in kind as the Divine Presence in Baptism is certainly not the Real Objective Presence which the Catholic Church holds and professes.

41. CRANMER'S METAPHORICAL USE OF THE TERM 'SACRIFICE.'

So much of Cranmer's metaphorical use of the term 'Real Presence.' Of the Sacrifice he says:

He [Dr. Richard Smith] belieth me in two things. . . . The one is that I deny the Sacrifice of the Mass, which in my book have most plainly set out the sacrifice of Christian people in the Holy Communion or Mass (if Dr. Smith will needs so term it).[1]

This, again, sounds satisfactory, and the passage has actually been quoted to prove that Cranmer believed in the Catholic doctrine of the Mass. But he continues:

And yet have I denied that it is a sacrifice propitiatory for sin, or that the priest alone maketh any sacrifice there. For it is the sacrifice of all Christian people to remember Christ's death, to laud and thank Him for it, and to publish it and shew it abroad unto other, to His honour and glory.

[1] *A Defence*, &c., p. 369 (*Answer to Dr. Smith's Preface*).

In another place he states the difference between the two kinds of sacrifice thus:

> One kind of sacrifice there is which is called **propitiatory** or merciful sacrifice, that is to say, such a sacrifice as pacifieth God's wrath and indignation, and obtaineth mercy and forgiveness for all our sins. . . . Another kind of sacrifice there is which doth not reconcile us to God, but is made of them which be reconciled by Christ, to testify our duties to God, and to shew ourselves thankful to Him. And therefore they call it the sacrifice of laud, praise, and thanksgiving.
>
> The first kind of sacrifice Christ offereth unto God for us; the second kind we offer to God by Christ. And by the first kind of sacrifice Christ offered also us unto His Father; and by the second we offer ourselves and all that we have unto Him and His Father. *And this sacrifice generally is our whole obedience unto God in keeping His laws and commandments.* . . .[1]

And presently adds:

> But all such priests as pretend to be Christ's successors in making a sacrifice of *him*, they be his most heinous and horrible adversaries. For never no man made a sacrifice of *Christ* but he himself only. . . . Forasmuch as he hath given *himself* to death for us, to be an oblation and sacrifice to his Father for our sins, let us give *ourselves* again to him, making unto him an oblation, not of goats, sheep, kine, and other beasts that have no reason, as was accustomed before Christ's coming, but of a creature that hath reason, that is *ourselves* . . . . mortifying the beastly and unreasonable affections that would gladly rule and reign in us. *These be the sacrifices of Christian men*, these hosts and oblations be acceptable to Christ.

And again:

> When the old Fathers called the Mass or Supper of the Lord a sacrifice, they meant that it was a sacrifice of lauds and thanksgiving (*and so as well the people as the priest do sacrifice*), or else that it was a remembrance of the very true sacrifice pre-

---

[1] *A Defence*, &c., pp. 346-49.

pitiatory of Christ; but they *meant in no wise that it is a very true sacrifice for sin*, and applicable by the priest for the living and the dead.[3]

From these various statements we see that although, to protect himself against the Patristic arguments of his opponents, Cranmer professed to believe in a sacrifice connected with Holy Communion, he resolves it into a sacrifice in which the person offering is not an earthly representative of Christ, or the thing offered the Body and Blood of Christ, but the offerers are the Christian people acting in their own name, and the thing offered is themselves, through their praise and thanksgiving for the benefit of redemption, their obedience to God's Law, and their subjugation of all evil passions. We also ourselves, following the example of Holy Scripture, call such things by the name of sacrifices, but they are metaphorical sacrifices, and absolutely distinct from the true and proper sacrifice which we acknowledge in the Mass. Nor is there anywhere in Cranmer's writings to be found any claim to believe in this last. On the contrary, as the passages already quoted show, to which an abundance of others might be added, for such a sacrifice he had nothing but loathing and invective.

42. CRANMER'S METAPHORICAL USE OF THE TERM 'PRIESTHOOD.'

As for the priesthood which offers, he has told us, both in these passages and likewise in some quoted a few pages higher up, that it is not confined to any one order of persons specially set apart, but is inherent in

---

[1] *A Defence*, &c., p. 351.

'all Christian people.' The same idea is more distinctly stated in another place:

> The humble confession of all penitent hearts, their acknowledgment of Christ's benefits, their thanksgiving for the same, their faith and consolation in the same, their humble submission and obedience to God's will and commandments, is a sacrifice of lauds and praise, accepted and allowed of God, no less than the sacrifice of the priest. For Almighty God, without respect of person, accepteth the oblation and sacrifice of priest and laymen, . . . of every man according to his faithful and obedient heart unto Him, and that through the sacrifice propitiatory of Jesu Christ.[1]

43. SIMILAR USE OF TERMS AMONG LATER ANGLICAN DIVINES.

As the Bull says, the circumstances of its origin have infused into the Anglican Ordinal a spirit or native character which has become a part of itself, and never can be separated from it. Hence its value would remain unaffected even if it could be shown that in later times the representative divines of your Communion held opinions more nearly approximating to the doctrines of the Catholic Church in regard to the triplet of connected truths of which we have been speaking. As a matter of fact, however, we submit to you—and probably you will not disagree with us—that, although within certain limits your standard writers have differed somewhat among themselves and perhaps formed schools, some holding what is called Higher and others what is called Lower doctrine, the range of their differences has never travelled substantially beyond the borders of the doctrinal statement we have obtained from Cranmer. Both schools have consistently dis-

[1] *A Defence*, &c., p. 352.

avowed belief in the Real Objective Presence and the sacrifice founded **upon that**. But one of them has laid stress on the acknowledgment of some kind of sacrifice in which the thing offered is the praise and devotion and self-surrender of the worshippers, or their alms and oblations, and in connection with which a bare commemoration (as the Council of Trent calls it) is made of the death and sacrifice of Calvary. And this Higher school often employs language—mostly when confronted with the similar language of the Fathers—which when isolated from **its context might** sound like an assertion of **the genuine Catholic doctrine.**

We may appeal, for **a** confirmation of **this** judgment, **to** the collection of passages from your great divines in **Dr.** Pusey's Tract 81 among the *Tracts for the Times*. His object there is to show that your Church has **all** along believed in a Eucharistic sacrifice, and he has naturally selected the authors whose writings best illustrate his position; and yet on examination they are found to contend only for the same kind of sacrifice as Cranmer. In Appendix VI. we have given a sufficient number of such passages to demonstrate this point. We may therefore be content here with two passages—one from **Waterland, the** other from Newman—which are valuable because **in** them these **well-**informed writers give us their **own** estimate of the prevalent opinions of Anglican writers on the point in question.

44. WATERLAND QUOTED.

Waterland, after discussing the opinions of divines previous **to** 1737, when he was writing, sums up the doctrine which he held himself and believed to have been taught **by them.**

The service, therefore, of the Eucharist on the foot of the ancient Church language is both a true and a proper sacrifice, . . . and the noblest that we are capable of offering, when considered as comprehending under it many a true and evangelical sacrifice: (1) the sacrifice of alms to the poor, and oblations to the Church, . . . not the material offering, . . . but the service; (2) the sacrifice of prayer; (3) the sacrifice of prayer and thanksgiving; (4) the sacrifice of a penitent and contrite heart; (5) the sacrifice of ourselves; (6) the offering of the mystical Body of Christ, that is, His Church; (7) the offering up of true converts or sincere penitents to God by their pastors; (8) the sacrifice of faith and hope and self-humiliation in commemorating the great sacrifice. . . .

From hence, likewise, may we understand in what sense the officiating authorised ministers perform the office of proper evangelical priests in this service. They do it in three ways: (1) as commemorating in solemn form the same sacrifice here below which Christ our High Priest commemorates above; (2) as handing up those prayers and those services of Christians to Christ our Lord, who, as High Priest, recommends the same in heaven to God Our Father; (3) as offering up to God all the faithful. . . . In these three ways the Christian officers are priests, or liturgs.[1]

45. CARDINAL NEWMAN'S ESTIMATE OF THE TEACHING OF THE GREAT ANGLICAN DIVINES.

Cardinal Newman, in his Preface to Mr. Hutton's *Anglican Ministry*, discusses this same question, and, quoting the above passage from Waterland, confirms its judgment with a judgment of his own based on his extensive acquaintance with the writings of Anglican divines. Cardinal Newman also testifies in the same Preface to the beliefs of those who were the contemporaries of his earlier years, naming 'Dr. Ogilvie, Mr. Hugh Rose, Dr. Lyall, Dr. Hook, Dr. Faussett, Mr. John

---

[1] *Works*, vol. vii. pp. 341-350. Oxford edition of 1830.

Miller, Bishop Selwyn, Bishop Wordsworth,' and 'Bishop Bethell, Bishop Van Mildert, Bishop Mant, Dr. Routh, and Dr. Collinson,' ' as being High Churchmen beyond others, and yet not dreaming that they possessed this gift' of consecrating and offering in the Catholic sense, and so presenting ' the most telling contrast with the professions and observances of the Ritualists.'

Cardinal Newman here contrasts the traditional Anglican doctrine with the recent doctrine of the extreme High Church section of your Communion; and since the days when he wrote the numbers of this party have grown considerably. We have no desire to question, any more than the Cardinal does, that many of these believe in a true Objective Presence, a true Sacrifice, and a true Sacrificial Priesthood. On the contrary we acknowledge willingly that their books, and still more their practices, bear indisputable testimony that they do. For we see that they lay stress on the worship of the Sacramental Presence, on non-communicant attendance (another name for hearing Mass), and on priestly power, while Cranmer and your older divines, together with the not inconsiderable number of their modern representatives, lay stress on the idolatry of Eucharistic adoration, and on the injury done to the perfect oblation on the Cross by the practice of private Masses. We may sympathise with this returning attraction for the Catholic doctrines; but, in view of the essentially different and opposite attitude towards them of your representative divines until recent times, we cannot admit that the modern beliefs of the extreme High Churchmen have any bearing on the interpretation of the language of your Ordinal.

46. CONCLUSION DRAWN.

A certain kind of sacrifice and priesthood, then, your Church, as represented by your standard divines, has persistently claimed to possess; it proves, however, on examination to be such, not in the literal and Catholic sense of the term, but only metaphorically. The human mind delights in tracing analogies, and it has been the custom in all ages to call the heart's self-surrender, with its offerings of praise and prayer and service, by the name of sacrifice, because these things are of the nature of gifts which involve cost to self. Scripture itself uses this language, and we are far, therefore, from objecting to it. On the contrary we employ it very generally ourselves. It is important, however, to bear in mind that figurative language is figurative, and not to confound resemblances with the realities. The true Sacrifice and Priesthood—that is to say, the Sacrifice in which the true Body and Blood of Christ is sacrificed and offered, and the Priesthood which is endowed with the power to consecrate and offer it—your Church, speaking through the same representatives, has, with equal persistency and in the most stringent terms, repudiated altogether.

And this is all that Leo XIII. has said in the passage above quoted, which you have pronounced to be 'harsh and inconsiderate.' When he says that he can find ' no clear mention in your whole Ordinal of the sacrifice, of consecration, of the *sacerdotium*, and of the power of consecrating and offering sacrifice,' but, on the contrary, finds that ' every trace of these things which had been, in such prayers of the Catholic rite as they [your Reformers] had not entirely rejected, was deliberately removed and **struck out,**' he **is o**bviously speaking, not of any metaphorical sacrifice and priesthood, but of the true sacrifice **and** priesthood which he had just previously defined. Now, therefore, that the confusion of terms has been removed we may return to his argument from the general character of your Ordinal. Since **the** makers of this Ordinal have not inserted in it any clear mention of the sacrifice and the priesthood, but, on the contrary, took pains to strike out all such references from those prayers which they took over from the ancient **rite**; since, moreover, we know from their writings, and from the writings of a succession of your leading divines, unbroken until the second quarter of this century, that these omissions and suppressions were made designedly, out of that downright hatred for the aforesaid doctrines which **has** been a characteristic note of your Church throughout—is there any fault to be found with Leo XIII.'s inference that your Ordinal cannot be deemed to signify definitely the conveyance of a sacrificial priesthood, and cannot therefore be a valid rite for that purpose?

47. WHAT IS THE DOCTRINE OF **THE 'RESPONSIO'** ON THE SACRIFICE AND PRIESTHOOD?

We come now to the last point on which we propose to touch. It is a question that we wish to put to you. Your modern beliefs concerning the sacrifice and the priesthood cannot of course afford a rule for the inter**pre**tation of **an** Ordinal drawn up three centuries ago. Still it is of interest to know what you take to be the doctrine of your Church in regard **to** these two points, and we have found the most important passage in your

WHAT IS THE DOCTRINE OF THE 'RESPONSIO'?

Reply to be that in which you make a statement on this subject (Section XI.). You will allow us to quote it here.

We truly teach the doctrine of the Eucharistic sacrifice, and do not believe it to be a 'nude commemoration of the Sacrifice of the Cross,' an opinion which seems to be attributed to us by the quotation from that Council [the Council of Trent]. But we think it sufficient in the Liturgy which we use in celebrating the Holy Eucharist, while lifting up our hearts to the Lord, and when now consecrating the gifts already offered, that they may become to us the Body and Blood of our Lord Jesus Christ, to signify the sacrifice which is offered at that point of the service in such terms as these. We continue a perpetual memory of the precious death of Christ, who is our Advocate with the Father and the propitiation for our sins, according to His precept, until His coming again. For first we offer the sacrifice of praise and thanksgiving; then next we plead and represent before the Father the Sacrifice of the Cross, and by it we confidently entreat remission of sins and all other benefits of the Lord's Passion for all the whole Church; and, lastly, we offer the sacrifice of ourselves to the Creator of all things which we have already signified by the oblations of His creatures. This whole action, in which the people has necessarily to take part with the priest, we are accustomed to call the Eucharistic sacrifice.

We confess that comparing this passage with the passages quoted above from Cranmer and Waterland, and the many similar passages given in Appendix VI. to this Letter, we have understood you to be expressing the same views as your standard writers; rejecting by implication the Real Objective Presence, the Sacrifice in which the true Body and Blood of Christ is the victim, and the Priesthood which claims to have received a specific spiritual power to offer such a sacrifice; but at the same time affirming and ascribing to your Church a sacrifice in which the thing offered is the congregation with its praise, its service, and its gifts, and claiming likewise for each individual, the layman as well as the clergyman, a metaphorical priesthood to correspond with this metaphorical sacrifice. The presumption was that you would adhere to the teaching of these authorities, and your words seem to us to confirm the presumption.

For the words in which you describe your Eucharistic sacrifice as consisting in the offering of praise and thanksgiving, and of the persons of the worshippers with their gifts to God's service, are in obvious agreement with the language of Cranmer and your other divines. Your reminder, too, that 'the people necessarily take part with the priest' in the offering of the sacrifice—especially when read in connection with the passage elsewhere which states (Section XIX.) that the priesthood, in contradistinction to the pastorate, 'is shared in some measure with the people'—seems to lean towards Cranmer's doctrine that 'the difference that is between priest and layman in this matter is only in the ministration.' On the other hand you carefully abstain from affirming belief in the Real Objective Presence of the Body and Blood of Christ and the sacrificial offering of That. Of course you do deny that you believe the Holy Eucharist 'to be a nude commemoration of the Sacrifice of the Cross'; meaning, however, by your denial, like Cranmer, as it seems, not that Our Lord is present in the Sacrament, but that the spiritual eating and drinking proper to the Sacrament is not bare of spiritual effect on the soul. 'I never said' (are his words) ' of the whole Supper that it is but a signification or a bare memory of Christ's death, but I teach that it is a spiritual refreshing wherein our souls be fed and nourished with Christ's very Flesh and Blood to eternal life.'[1] You do besides no doubt tell us that you 'consecrate the gifts already offered that they may become to us the Body and Blood of Our Lord Jesus Christ.' But this phrase also, which is somewhat inaccurately quoted from your First Prayer Book, you seem to be using in Cranmer's sense, which he has expounded to us in the passage already quoted. No doubt both these phrases might be understood in a more Catholic sense. But it appears inconceivable that, if you had really wished to ascribe to your Church belief in a Real Objective Presence you would have failed to say so with the utmost distinctness, for this is the very turning point of the whole question.

48. A QUESTION PUT TO THE ARCHBISHOPS.

On the other hand, it is notorious that many members of your Communion have understood you in this passage to be affirming the doctrine of a Real Objective Presence and of the Sacrifice founded on that, and it is this dispute about your meaning which moves us to ask you a question. It seems to us that, as the object of your Letter was to make plain for all time the doctrine of your Church on the subject of Holy Orders, and this point about the Real Presence and the true Sacrifice lies at the very roots of that controversy, we are entitled to ask you to remove the doubt which has arisen in the way described, and tell us in unmistakable terms what your real meaning is.

If, then, we have mistaken your meaning in the passage referred to, will you frankly say so? But

---

[1] *A Defence*, &c., p. 148.

if we have understood you rightly, we must claim your reply as tantamount to an acknowledgment that the Bull has not misjudged the character of your Ordinal. It will remain, of course, that you have dissented from its pronouncements on many other points; but in regard to this, the most crucial point of all, it will be made clear that in your judgment as well as in that of Leo XIII. your Ordinal was never intended, and was therefore never fitted, to make sacrificing priests in the strict sense of the term.

49. THE DOCTRINE OF THE ORIENTALS ON THE SACRIFICE AND PRIESTHOOD.

One word, before concluding, on a matter which has been very much before your minds of late. We have not entered into the question of your agreement with the Eastern or Russian Communion, for it has not come within the direct scope of this Letter. But we may point out that in all which concerns the Real Objective Presence, the true Propitiatory Sacrifice, and the nature and extent of the Priesthood, the Church over which Leo XIII. rules and the great Eastern or Russian Church hold identical doctrine. The object of Leo XIII. in his Bull has really been to defend the doctrine held in common by East and West, and you cannot reject the doctrine of Leo. XIII. without at the same time rejecting that of the East. On this point it will be sufficient to refer you to the language of the Synod of Bethehem, for which see Appendix VII.

50. CONCLUDING WORDS.

In concluding this Letter it is a real pleasure to us to find in your own concluding paragraph so much to which we can subscribe. You 'wish it to be known to all men how zealous you are in your devotion to peace and unity,' and you pray that 'even from this controversy there may grow fuller knowledge of the truth, greater patience, and a broader desire for peace in the Church of Christ, the Saviour of the world.' Nor can we forget, as we read these words, that on a still more recent and most impressive occasion you have declared 'the Divine purpose of visible unity amongst Christians to be a fact of revelation,' and a fact which in these days we should 'take every opportunity to emphasise.' Here at least is common ground on which we can meet. We go beyond you, indeed, in holding firmly that visible unity is of the essence, not of the well-being only, of the Catholic Church, but we are in accord with you in bewailing the sad spectacle of division among Christians, and recognising it to be most opposed to the revealed purpose of God. We are in accord with you as to the importance of declining to be led by mere national or personal tastes and proclivities, but 'of turning towards our Lord Jesus Christ and weighing patiently what He intended when He established the ministry of His Gospel.' And oh! that the happy day might come when you could be in accord with us also in perceiving that the secret of visible unity is to be sought, not in the system which during its comparatively short-lived existence has been the fertile mother of division, but rather in that system which has stood firm through the ages, holding the nations **together in a** unity so conspicuous as to excite admiration even where it **fails** to secure **obedience.**

We are
Your Graces' Servants in Christ,

HERBERT CARDINAL VAUGHAN,
Archbishop of Westminster.
✠ WILLIAM, *Bishop of Plymouth.*
✠ JOHN CUTHBERT, *Bishop of Newport.*
✠ EDWARD, *Bishop of Nottingham.*
✠ EDWARD, *Bishop of Birmingham.*
✠ RICHARD, *Bishop of Middlesborough.*
✠ ARTHUR, *Bishop of Northampton.*
✠ JOHN, *Bishop of Portsmouth.*
✠ THOMAS, *Bishop of Hexham & Newcastle.*
✠ WILLIAM, *Bishop of Leeds.*
✠ JOHN, *Bishop of Salford.*
✠ WILLIAM, *Bishop of Clifton.*
✠ THOMAS, *Bishop of Liverpool.*
✠ FRANCIS, *Bishop of Southwark.*
✠ SAMUEL, *Bishop of Shrewsbury.*
✠ FRANCIS, *Bishop of Ascalon, V.A. of Wales.*

Feast of St. Thomas, Archbishop of Canterbury and Martyr, 1897.
Archbishop's House, Westminster.

APPENDICES

I

The Faculties of Julius III. (see p. 14).

IT is suggested in the *Responsio* that there were other letters of Julius III. which should have been produced and considered, since without them it is impossible to know what rule in dealing with Edwardine orders Pole was desired to follow : 'Where (it is asked) are the faculties granted to Pole after August 5, 1553, and before March 8, 1554, which Julius confirms in his letter of the latter date, to be "freely used" in respect of Orders received with any irregularity or failure in the accustomed form, but does not detail and define? Without these faculties the "rules of action" to be observed by Pole are imperfectly known.' (Section VI.) This suggestion, however, is founded only on a misreading of the Brief of March 8, 1554. The clause in question runs thus: '*Nos causam tuæ subsistentiæ in eisdem partibus approbantes circumspectioni tuæ quod . . . omnibus et singulis prædictis et quibusvis aliis tibi concessis, et quæ per præcedentes tibi conceduntur facultatibus . . . uti possis . . . libere uti . . . possis, plenam et liberam apostolicam auctoritatem per præsentes concedimus facultatem et potestatem.*' ('We approving the cause of your waiting in those parts grant to your prudence by these presents full and free apostolical authority, faculty, and power . . . to use . . . to use freely all and each of the aforesaid faculties, and any others which may have been granted you, and likewise those which are granted you by these presents.') Here the 'all and each of the aforesaid faculties' are those specified and given in the Bull of the previous August 5, and it is these and the others 'granted by these presents' (*i.e.* by the

Brief itself) to which the extension of the Brief of March 8 directly refers. The phrase 'any others which may have been granted you' is merely the safeguarding phrase which it is usual to insert in Bulls and similar legal documents. So far as the clause goes it cannot be gathered that there were in reality any such 'other faculties,' although we can otherwise certify ourselves of the existence of some. But there is no reason to suppose that any of them dealt with the question of orders, and in any case the argument which Leo XIII. constructs from the two letters of Julius III., when taken together with the other above-mentioned instruments, is an argument conclusive in itself independently of support from other sources.

II

The Instruction for the Armenians of Eugenius IV. (see p. 36).

It is stated in the *Responsio* (Section VI.) that Leo XIII. 'seems wholly to forget Eugenius's Decree, which he has silently thrown over in another part of his letter.' The reference is to the Decree of Eugenius IV. on behalf of the Armenians whom that Pope had just united to the Church in the Council of Florence. To this Decree is appended an Instruction on the Sacraments taken from the writings of St. Thomas of Aquin, and in the Instruction the following clause occurs:

The sixth sacrament is that of Order: the matter of which is the thing by the delivery of which the Order is conferred: as, for instance, the order of the presbyterate is conferred by the delivery of the chalice with wine and the paten with bread: the diaconate by the giving of the book of the Gospels. . . . The form of the priesthood is as follows: Receive the power of offering sacrifice in the Church for the living and the dead. In the name of the Father, &c.

The suggestion in the *Responsio* is that, whereas in this clause Eugenius defined that delivery of the instruments and not imposition of hands is the matter of the Sacrament of Orders, Leo XIII., although he perceived that this decision of his predecessor was erroneous, and has given a decision inconsistent with it, had not the candour to acknowledge openly so important a fact, but tried to conceal it under the veil of silence.

All this, however, is misapprehension. Leo XIII. has given no decision inconsistent with the Instruction on behalf of the Armenians; and if he has been silent about the existence of this Instruction, his silence is easily explained. He was silent about it because no occasion arose when a reference to it would have been in point. As has been expounded in the text, the case on behalf of the Anglican Ordinal broke down in the very first stage, whereas the Instruction *pro Armenis* could not affect it unless and until it reached the second stage. In other words, the first point to be ascertained in reference to the Anglican Ordinal was whether it contained at least some combination of ceremony and accompanying form so constructed as to signify definitely the sacramental grace to be imparted. On this point the Instruction *pro Armenis* had no bearing whatever, but it was the only point that proved to need investigation, since its investigation terminated in the unhesitating conclusion that the Anglican rite did not satisfy even that elementary requirement. Had the Anglican rite, however, passed successfully through this initial stage, by proving itself to bear a definite signification, it would have become necessary to inquire, in the next place, whether it fulfilled the further requirement of embodying its definite signification in that precise matter and form which had the sanction of Our Lord's positive appointment. And here the Instruction *pro Armenis* would have had to be considered along with the question whether Our Lord Himself fixed *in specie*, as the theologians say, the matter and form of this sacrament, or whether He merely promised to ratify the determination of His Church.

This being so, it is not really necessary to say anything more about the Instruction *pro Armenis*, and yet it may be convenient to explain in a few words its bearing on the Sacrament of Order, as interpreted by Catholic theologians. There are two opinions current among them as to its meaning and import. Some hold that its words must be taken in their obvious sense, and that we are to gather from them that delivery of instruments is truly the essential element of the Sacrament. Those who take this view, being well aware that there is no such ceremony in any Oriental rite except the Armenian itself—which perhaps adopted **it only** in deference to the Instruction—further hold that Our Lord Himself merely prescribed that the rite of Holy Orders should consist of some words and ceremonies distinctly signifying the sacramental grace, and left the determination of these ceremonies, as He certainly left the determination of the words, to be made by His Church according to her discretion—which discretion she might exercise differently in different times and places, as in fact she had prescribed delivery of the instruments in the West but not in the East. The other opinion as to the purport of the Instruction is that of those who hold that Eugenius IV. could not possibly have intended to declare delivery of the instruments to be essential for validity since otherwise he must necessarily have enforced the same not only on the Armenians but also upon the Greeks; which, however, he had not done, although in the very same Council of Florence he had reunited them to the Church after a careful examination into all their formularies and rites. These theologians therefore infer that the document containing the perplexing words was not intended to be more than a practical instruction showing what was customary in the Western Church, and even thus confining itself to the chief things. Eugenius, in fact, calls it a *brevissima formula*, which may account for its silence in regard to imposition of hands, without driving us into the violent hypothesis that this ceremony was deemed to be of minor consequence. It should be borne in mind, too, that the Instruction was not a composition drawn up at the time, but is an abridgment of an *opusculum* of St. Thomas much used at the time. St. Thomas was thus its real author, and St. Thomas leaves us under no doubt that he regarded imposition of hands as of co-ordinate importance with delivery of the instruments.[1]

Between these two opinions it is not necessary now to choose. It suffices to say that the second opinion has become by far the more common of the two, but that in the doubt whether the first opinion may not after all be the true one, it has been, is, and will probably continue to be our practice to reordain conditionally in the Western Church, whenever it is found that delivery of the instruments has been omitted. It is to this custom that Leo XIII. refers in the *Apostolicæ Curæ* when commenting on the decision in the Gordon case. Clearly, then, Leo XIII.'s

---

[1] Cp. *Sum. Theol.* 3ᵃ, q. xxxvii. art. 5 corp.

condemnation of Anglican Orders can in no sense be attributed, as the above quoted clause of the *Responsio* suggests, to any disregard of the Decree on behalf of the Armenians. On the contrary, if it be true that this Decree is an infallible definition and that it declares delivery of the instruments to be the one indispensable matter of the Sacrament, it only follows that besides the reasons actually urged by the recent Bull, there was also this other of the most palpable kind, which requires any Catholic authority to treat Anglican Orders as absolutely null and void.

III

The Resolution in the Abyssinian Case of 1704 (*see* p. 45).

It is alleged that in 1704 the Holy See decided that the words *Accipe Spiritum Sanctum*, if said concomitantly with imposition of hands, are of themselves a sufficient form for the conveyance of priestly orders. Such a decision, if genuine, would doubtless be inconsistent with the first, though not with the second, of the two arguments in the *Apostolicæ Curæ* by which the insufficiency of the Anglican form is established. The nature, however, of the so-called decision of 1704 has been misunderstood. The facts are as follows, stated briefly.

The Prefect Apostolic of Ethiopia, in 1704, represented that the schismatic Abouna of the Abyssinians held his ordinations, to the disregard of the ancient rite of his Church, in a very careless manner. He ordained the candidates by thousands at a time, passing rapidly in front of them, laying his episcopal cross, but not his hands, on the heads of those presented for the diaconate, and saying only the words *Accipe Spiritum Sanctum* whilst laying hands on those presented for the priesthood. Seeing that occasionally schismatic Abyssinian priests were received into the Catholic Church, the Prefect Apostolic inquired how orders thus imparted should be dealt with. The case was referred in the usual manner by the Congregation of the Holy Office to one of its Consultors, Padre Damasceno, and in due course the latter delivered his opinion, one clause of which ran thus:—'The ordination of a priest with imposition of hands and the pronouncement of the form as stated in the doubt [propounded] is valid, but the ordination of the deacon with the mere imposition of the patriarchal cross is altogether invalid.' This clause of the Consultor's Resolution when submitted to Clement XI., seemed to His Holiness unsafe, and accordingly he rejected it, writing against it in the margin *Dilata ad mentem*—' Left to stand over for the reason [privately] given.'[1]

As Clement XI. rejected P. Damasceno's Resolution, no sound argument in favour of the Anglican position can be drawn from it; but by some unexplained misadventure this Resolution found its way into the appendix of Antoine's treatise *De Ordine* in his *Moral Theology*, where it is set down as being, not what it really is, the rejected Resolution of a Consultor, but as the authentic Response of the Holy Office itself. Nor did the evil end there. In 1860 a somewhat similar application was made to the Holy Office by Mgr. Athanasius Kusam, Vicar Apostolic of the Copts, for guidance in dealing with converts whose orders had been received from the schismatic prelates in those parts. The text of the new application is given in Estcourt, App. XXXIV., and in *De Hierarchia Anglicana*, App. VI.; and it is necessary to notice an important difference between its tenor and that of the previous application of 1704. In the application of 1860 it is stated that the priesthood (not the diaconate) had been given without any imposition of hands, but solely with the imposition of a silver cross and an insufflation to which the words *Accipe Spiritum Sanctum* were annexed. The answer of the Holy Office to this *dubium* was, as might have been expected, 'Ordination [given] in the manner stated is invalid;' and it must be observed that this is the only *decision* then given in regard to these Coptic orders. But the Congregation added, by way of confirmation, 'Let there be given [to the Vicar Apostolic] the answer, dated April 9, 1704, of this Sacred Congregation of the Supreme Inquisition.' The 'answer' thus directed to be given

---

[1] F. Brandi in his *Roma e Canterbury* (p. 45) has given the full text of P. Damasceno's Resolution, together with a facsimile of the clause in question and of the marginal note appended to it by Clement XI. See also F. Brandi's Appendices xx.–xxiii. for other important documents bearing on this case.

was the very Resolution of 1704 which, as has been explained, was not an answer of the Congregation, but merely the rejected draft Resolution of its Consultor. Obviously this was an oversight, due apparently to Antoine's citation having been accepted as genuine without sufficient verification,[1] and being an oversight cannot be reasonably made into a ground of argument, the more so as the clause in this Resolution for the sake of which it was cited in 1860 was, **not the** clause in which **imposition** of hands with the words *Accipe Spiritum Sanctum* was pronounced to be sufficient, but the **clause in which** imposition of the bishop's cross with the said words was **pronounced to be** insufficient.

For these reasons we are clearly entitled to dismiss this Abyssinian 'Resolution' as having no bearing on the question of Anglican Orders. There is, however, a still remaining element of obscurity about the case, which, for its historic interest, may be touched on briefly. Seeing that Padre Damasceno must have been familiar with the practice of the Church, which offered no precedent for accepting Orders conferred by a form so indefinite, how could he have even ventured to suggest that *Accipe Spiritum Sanctum* was a sufficient form? Might he not **have** been expected at least **to** postulate that an exhaustive inquiry should be instituted to determine on the safety of **the** startling new departure he was recommending? Now there is in the Inquisition Archives an 'ancient *Relation* sent **to** the Supreme Congregation **by the Prefect** Apostolic of the **Copts**'[2] which **seems to** suggest **a** satisfactory explanation of this difficulty:

When (says this *Relation*) **there are many to** be ordained—for instance, twenty **or** thirty—the Bishop does not lay his hand upon the head of all, but holds it stretched out a little above their heads without touching them, and recites **the form** for all together. Then, before giving them the Communion in both kinds, he puts his two hands upon the two cheeks of each, and blows three times upon his face and mouth, saying in Coptic *Ci imbneuma csuab*, i.e. *Accipe Spiritum Sanctum*.

If Padre Damasceno had **a similar mode of** conferring orders brought under his notice, his Resolution—'*Ordinatio presbyteri cum manuum impositione et formæ prolatione prout in dubio est*

---

[1] See Franzelin's *votum* in *Roma e Canterbury*, p. 83.
[2] Brandi, *A Last Word on Anglican Ordinations*, p. 98.

valida'—is quite intelligible, for he will then have meant by '*prout in dubio*' the entire complex rite, and he will have taken the short rite with *Accipe Spiritum Sanctum* as sufficing in the sense that it indicated definitely who precisely were the candidates to whom the non-contactual extension of hands had been intended to refer.

And that he had this complex rite in mind may perhaps be gathered from his previous *votum*, which was laid before Clement XI. on February 14, 1704. For in this previous *votum* he had answered '*Quatenus Æthiopes Jacobitarum vel alio ritu utantur in quo eorum sacerdotes et monachi per manuum impositionem* **ordinentur**, *eorum ordinatio est valida.*' At that earlier date, then, he supposed that a form such as is found in the Coptic Pontifical had been employed. But Clement XI. having directed that further inquiries should be made, the Prefect Apostolic sent in the account ('Nell' Etiopica essendo necessità,' &c.), which in Canon Estcourt's Appendix XXXIV. figures at the head of the Resolution of April 10, 1704, in its published form. Hence the question arises, was the *dubium* to which Padre Damasceno refers in this Resolution of April 10, when he says '*Ordinatio prout in dubio*' &c., solely and exclusively this paragraph in Canon Estcourt's Appendix, or was it the *dubium* of his previous Resolution of February 14, as supplemented by this further information? The latter supposition seems probable enough in itself, though the documents as yet published do not make it certain.

But with these data before us we can understand the answer, based on Franzelin's *votum* of that year, which Cardinal Patrizi gave in his letter to Cardinal Manning of April 30, 1875:[1]

> From the Coptic rite itself, which is to be seen in their Pontificals, it is clear that the words *Accipe Spiritum Sanctum* do not constitute its entire form, nor is the sense of the document of 1704 which has been brought forward—but which is not a Decree of the Holy Office, as its Register shows—to be otherwise understood than as asserting that the ordination among the Copts, with the imposition of hands and the pronouncing of the form contained in their ancient rite, is to be deemed valid.

---

[1] *Ap.* Gasparri, *De Sacris Ordinationibus*, ii. 244.

IV.

The Essential Forms of the Ancient Ordination Rites (see p. 47).

In each of the rites which the Catholic Church has recognised the 'essential form' is contained in a 'consecrating prayer' to accompany the imposition of hands, and these prayers are all cast in the same type, defining in some way or other the Order to which the candidate is being promoted, and beseeching God to bestow upon him the graces necessary in his new state. This may be seen from the following table, which gives the clauses to this effect in the consecratory prayers of every rite which can colourably claim to have been at any time recognised as sufficient by the Catholic Church: namely, the Roman (as found in the ancient Leonine Sacramentary, and still preserved in the modern Pontifical), the Greek, the Syro-Maronite (which is also that of the Syro-Jacobites), the Nestorian, the Armenian, the Coptic (or Alexandro-Jacobite), and the Abyssinian; and together with these the Ancient Gallican rite (or what is conjecturally such), the rite in the Apostolical Constitutions, and that in the 'Canons of St. Hippolytus.'

The Roman Form (from the Leonine Sacramentary).

For the Diaconate.	For the Priesthood.	For the Episcopate.
Look down favourably, we beseech Thee, O Lord, on this Thy servant, whom we humbly dedicate to the *office of the Diaconate*, that he may serve at Thy Holy Altars. . . . Send down upon him, we beseech Thee, the Holy Spirit, that he may be strengthened by the sevenfold gift of Thy grace for the faithful discharge of the work of his ministry.	Grant, we beseech Thee, Almighty Father, to these Thy servants the *dignity of the Priesthood (presbyterii)*. . . May they so obtain from Thee, O Lord, the *office of second dignity* that it may be accepted by Thee.	Grant, therefore, to these Thy servants whom Thou hast called to the ministry of the High Priesthood (*summi sacerdotii*) this grace, that whatever was signified in those garments by the brightness of gold . . . may shine in the life and conduct of these men; fulfil in Thy priests (*sacerdotibus*) the *perfection* (*summam*) of Thy mystery *al.* ministry). . . . Grant to them the *throne of the Episcopate* to rule Thy Church.

The Greek Form (*from* Goar's '*Euchologium*').

For the Diaconate.

Do Thou, O Lord, preserve this man, whom it hath pleased Thee to have promoted by me to the *office of the Diaconate*. . . . Bestow upon him the grace which was granted to thy protomartyr *Stephen*, the first called to the work of this *ministry* (διακονίας).

For the Priesthood.

O God . . . who hast adorned with the name of *priest* (πρεσβυτέρου) those who have been deemed worthy *in that grade* to sanctify the word of Thy Truth, do Thou, the Lord of all, be pleased to grant that he whom it hath pleased Thee should be *promoted* by me, shall *receive this great grace* of Thy Spirit in innocency of life and unfailing faith.

For the Episcopate.

O Lord, Our God, who through Thy renowned apostle Paul didst sanction a *series of grades and Orders* to serve and minister at Thy venerable and spotless mysteries on the Holy Altar. Having appointed, first, apostles, then prophets, then doctors, do Thou, O Lord of all, confirm **by the coming and power and grace of Thy Holy Spirit this** man who has been elected by votes and accounted worthy to receive the evangelical yoke and the *Pontifical dignity* (ἀρχιερατικῆς ἀξίας) at the hands of me, a sinner, and the ministers and fellow-bishops who are standing by. . . . Make also his *pontificate* blameless.

The Maronite Form (*from* Denzinger's '*Ritus Orientales*').

Look, O Lord, upon Thy servant and send down upon him the grace of the Holy Spirit; . . . **and** as Thou didst give grace to *Stephen*, the first whom Thou didst call to this *ministry* (διακονίαν), so grant that Thine aid from heaven may come down also on this Thy servant.

Choose him by Thy grace, and through Thy mercy promote this Thy servant who, because of Thy great kindness and the gift of Thy Divine grace, is presented to-day **(that** he may be **raised)** from the Order of **deacons to the high and sublime grade of** *priests*. Grant to him, O Lord, that he may excel in goodness of life and may stand blameless and minister without sin at Thy altar.

Perfect Thy grace and **Thy** gift in us and in this Thy servant and *Bishop* . . . and grant him, O Lord God, **together with this imposition of hands, which** to-day he receives from Thee, the influx of Thy Holy Spirit; and make him worthy to obtain mercy from Thee to **perform his** priesthood and offer Thee pure sacrifices. . . .

The Nestorian Form (*from Denzinger*).

For the Diaconate.

O Lord God ... who hast chosen Thy Holy Church, and hast raised up in it prophets and apostles and priests and doctors ... and hast placed in it also *deacons* for the ministry of Thy mysteries ... and as Thou didst choose *Stephen* and his companions, so now, O Lord, according to Thy mercy, grant to these Thy servants the grace of the Holy Spirit, that they may be chosen *deacons*, and may minister at Thy Altar, ... and may shine in works of justice.

For the Priesthood.

Do Thou, O great God of power, ... look down now on these Thy servants, and choose them with a holy choosing through the indwelling of Thy holy Spirit, ... and elect them to the *Priesthood*, Lord God of strength, that they may lay their hands on the sick and heal them, ... and with purity of heart and good conscience **may** serve Thy **Holy Altar, offering to Thee the oblations of** prayer **and the sacrifices of confessions.** ...

For the Episcopate.

O **Great God** ... who by the **Blood** of our Lord Jesus Christ hast acquired to Thyself Thine Holy Church, and hast constituted in her prophets, and apostles, and doctors, and priests. ... Do Thou, **O** Lord, **now also cause** Thy **face to shine on this** Thy servant, and choose him by a holy choosing, that he may be to Thee **a** *perfect priest* who may emulate the true High Priest who laid down His life for us. Give him power from on high ... **that by virtue of** his gift he *may make priests and deacons.* ...

The Armenian Form (*from Denzinger*).

O Lord God ... who hast appointed in it *deacons* for the ministry of Thy Holy Church, ... look down propitiously ... on this Thy servant who is ordained now to the *ministry* of Thy Church. ... Give him the power and grace of blessed Stephen, Thy first martyr and first *deacon*, that filled with the Holy Ghost he may remain spotless in the ministry of Thy Holy Table (*Denzinger*).

Hear, O Lord, now the voice of our prayers, and this Thy servant, whom Thou hast elected and received to the *Priesthood*, being now ordained, do Thou strengthen in this *Priesthood* to which he is called; ... grant him the Apostolic grace to **put to** flight and dispel **all deadly diseases** ... **to call down the Holy Spirit from heaven for the life of the regenerate** ... to consecrate the awful and Holy Sacrament of the Body and Blood of Our Lord and Saviour Jesus Christ ... in fine to fulfil perfectly and holily every work of his *Priesthood* (*Denzinger*).

The prayer of [Episcopal] ordination is very long, but constructed on the same lines as those for deacons and priests, and contains **the** petition:

'Elect him **with a** holy election **that he** may be a *perfect priest*. ... **Clothe him** with power that ... through the power **of Thy** gifts he may **make** priests, and deacons, subdeacons and deaconesses. ... Perfect the souls of those over whom he is made *Bishop*.' [From 'The current Quarterly Paper of the Archbishops' Mission,' ap. the *Guardian*, April 21, 1897, p. 600.]

The Coptic Form (*from Denzinger*).

For the Diaconate.

Cause **Thy** face **to** shine on Thy servant ... who is promoted **to the** *Diaconate* by **the vote and judgment** of those **who have** brought him here. Fill him with **the** Holy Spirit and wisdom and power, **as** Thou didst fill *Stephen* the first *deacon* and first martyr. ... Make him *minister* **of** Thy **Holy** Altar, **that** he **may minister according to** Thy good pleasure in the office of *deacon*.

For the Priesthood.

Look down on Thy servant ... who is promoted to the *Priesthood* according to the vote and judgment of those. Fill him with the Holy Spirit and with grace as he stands in fear before Thy face that he may rule Thy people with a pure heart. ... May he fulfil the works of the priesthood over Thy people.

For the Episcopate.

Pour out the power of Thy *ruling* spirit [or 'spirit of rule,' Gr. ἡγεμονικόν] which Thou didst give to Thine apostles in Thy **name.** Grant then this **same** grace **to Thy servant** ... whom **Thou hast** *chosen to be Bishop*, that he may feed Thy holy flock. Let him have power of forgiving **sins** according to the command of the Only Begotten Son, Our Lord Jesus Christ, and *constituting clergy* for the sanctuary. ...

The Abyssinian Form as **copied by** *Mgr. Bel from some Abyssinian Books and sent to Canon* **Estcourt** *(Estcourt, App. XXXV.).*

Send down the spirit of goodness and watchfulness on this Thy servant whom Thou hast chosen that he may be a *deacon* in Thy Church.

Look down on this Thy servant; grant that he may receive spiritual grace and the counsel of sanctity, that with purity of heart he may direct Thy people even **as** Thou didst bid Moses to **choose** *leaders* **for** Thy chosen **people, and** fill **him with the Holy** Spirit which Thou didst ive to Moses.[1]

O God who hast never left Thy Church without ministers, ... pour out Thy Holy Spirit on this Thy servant, whom Thou hast assumed to the *Episcopate* that he may **guard** Thy flock. ... and offer the acceptable **victim to** Thee in the Church ... bestow the Holy Spirit on **the** priests, together **with** the power of forgiving sins and administering Sacraments.

---

[1] This Abyssinian form for the priesthood is the solitary exception of which it might possibly be said that the character of the order imparted is not stated in the essential form. But as regards this, it must be remembered that we have it not direct from the Abyssian Pontifical, and a clause like those in the forms for the diaconate and the episcopate, ' Whom Thou hast assumed to the priesthood,' may have dropped out. However, in any case the Holy See has never acknowledged the sufficiency of this Abyssinian form.

THE ESSENTIAL FORMS OF ANCIENT RITES

Ancient Gallican Form (*from the Gelasian Sacramentary*).

For the Diaconate.
(*Conjectured.*)

Deign to look **with** special favour on **this** Thy servant, that being set apart for Thy worship he may become a pure *minister* at Thy Holy Altars, and **made** purer by Thy pardon; may he be counted worthy of *the **grade** of those* whom **Thy** apostles chose in sevenfold number *with* **blessed** Stephen for their leader and chief.

For the Priesthood.
(*Conjectured.*)

Pour out, O Lord, from Thine **hand** Thy benediction (*manum benedictionis tuæ*) on these Thy servants whom we dedicate to the honour of the *Priesthood* ... May they **for the** service of Thy people transform (the bread and wine) into the Body and Blood **of** Thy Son by their immaculate benediction.

For the Episcopate.
(*Lost.*)

The Form in the *Apostolic Constitutions*.[1]

Cause Thy countenance to shine on this Thy servant elected **to** Thy ministry (διακονίαν), and fill him with the Holy Spirit and power, **even** as Thou didst fill Stephen, Thy protomartyr.

Do Thou **also** look **now upon Thy servant** who by **the vote and** judgment of the entire clergy has been enrolled in the *Order of Priests*, and fill him with the spirit of grace and counsel ... even as Thou didst look upon Thy chosen race, and **didst** order **Moses to** choose *seniors* whom Thou didst fill with Thy Spirit.

Grant in Thy name, O Searcher of Hearts, to this Thy servant whom Thou hast chosen to the *Episcopate* that he may feed Thy holy flock and fulfil the office of his Pontificate holily before Thee, ministering to Thee day and night, ... offering to Thee without blame the pure and unbloody sacrifice which Thou didst institute through **Christ**.

The Form in the '*Canons of Hippolytus*.'

O God, ... pour out Thy Holy Spirit on **Thy** servant ... and prepare him along with those **who** *minister* to Thee according **to** Thy good pleasure, even as *Stephen* did.... Accep all his *service*.

O God, ... by whose command it is that from **Adam** there should **descend a** just **race** through this *priest*, who is the great Abraham, ... look down on Thy servant ... granting him Thy strength and the spirit of power which Thou didst bestow on Thy holy apostles; ... grant him, O Lord, the *Priesthood*.

[The **same as** for the Priesthood, except that **the word** 'Bishop' is substituted for 'Priest' wherever it occurs.]

---

[1] These two last-mentioned rites are only known to us as literary remains.

H

V

Opinions of Cranmer's Colleagues on the Mass (see p. 64).

Knowing Cranmer's own beliefs, and seeing how predominant was his influence over the composition and authorisation of your Prayer Book and Ordinal, we might dispense ourselves from the task of collecting passages to show the opinion of his colleagues. 'Nothing,' says Strype, 'was admitted into that liturgy without his leave, and nothing was rejected or impeded [from admission into it] which he judged proper to insert.'[1] The Zürich letters testify to the same effect in many places, whilst the original copies of the liturgy are found to be either in his handwriting or else annotated by him, and are unanimously ascribed to him. Still, as it will help to demonstrate how entirely the Prayer Book and Ordinal were the outcome of his views, it may be well to add quotations from some of the other prelates and divines who assisted in the composing or authorising of these formularies, and have left us a record of their beliefs. Thus:

NICHOLAS RIDLEY, who was Cranmer's lieutenant in the sad campaign, and whose influence was only less than that of his chief, has expressed his mind in the same sense as Cranmer in many places. Out of these may be selected one from the *Brief Declaration* against Transubstantiation, written during his imprisonment, which states the point at issue between the Catholics and his own party with the utmost clearness.

What is the matter of the sacrament, whether it is the natural substance of bread, or the natural substance of Christ's own body? [It should be noticed that he recognises no third possibility.]

The truth of this question, truly tried out and agreed upon, no doubt will cease the controversy in all the rest. For if it be Christ's own natural body, born of the Virgin, then assuredly . . . they must needs grant transubstantiation, that is a change of the substance of bread into the substance of Christ's body; then also they must grant the carnal and corporal presence of Christ's body; then must the sacrament be adored with the honour due unto Christ Himself . . . then if the priest do offer the sacrament, he doth offer Christ Himself. . . .

---
[1] *Memorials*, i. 302.

Now, on the other side, if . . . it be found that the substance of bread is the material substance of **the sacrament;** although, *for the change of the use office and dignity of the bread, the bread indeed sacramentally is changed* into the body of Christ, *as the water in Baptism is sacramentally* changed into the fountain of regeneration, and yet the material substance thereof remaineth all one as was before . . . *then must it follow* . . . *that there is but one material substance* in the sacrament of the body, and one only likewise in the sacrament of the blood; that there is no such thing as transubstantiation . . . [that] then also the natural **substance** of Christ's human nature, which He took of the Virgin Mary, is in heaven where it remaineth now in glory, and not here enclosed under the form of bread; then that godly honour . . . is not done unto the holy sacrament . . . finally then *doth it follow that Christ's blessed body and blood,* which was once only offered and shed upon the cross, being available for the sins of the whole world, *is offered up no more in the natural substance thereof, neither by the priest nor any other thing.*

Having thus shown that all else depends on the underlying question whether Christ's Body or the bread and wine is the 'material **substance of the sacrament**,' he presently tells us which of these **two alternatives he himself adopts**:

I do plainly affirm and say, that the *second* answer . . . I am persuaded to be the very true meaning and sense of God's holy word: that **is, that the natural** substance of the bread and wine is the true material substance **of** the **holy** sacrament of the blessed body and blood of our Saviour Christ.

Before, however, he reaches this point he inserts a paragraph to protest that upholders (like himself) of this second opinion must not be charged with denying 'simply and absolutely the presence of Christ's body and blood' in the sacrament. In this **paragraph** he explains himself just in the same way as Cranmer, **alleging that he** holds a presence *by grace,* and that such a 'presence' is deserving of the name of presence.

Now, then you will say, what kind of presence do they grant, and what do they deny? Briefly they deny the presence of Christ's body in the natural substance of his real and assumed nature, and *grant the presence* of the same *by grace*: that is, they affirm and say that the substance of the natural body and blood of Christ is only remaining in heaven, and so shall be unto the latter day . . . [but] by grace, I say, that is, by the gift of this life mentioned in St. John, and the properties of the same meet for our pilgrimage here on earth, the same body of Christ is here **present** with us. *Even as,* for example, we say *the same sun, which, in substance, never removeth his place out of the heavens, is yet present here by his beams, light, and natural influence,* when it shineth upon **the** earth. For God's word and his sacraments be, as it were, the beams of Christ.[1]

This quotation covers the ground, but besides it we have the explicit statement made by Cranmer at his trial at Oxford that he had been converted from Lutheran to Zwinglian views on the Sacrament by the persuasions of Ridley.

And against the doctrine of the Mass Ridley was equally unsparing in his denunciations. In this same work, for instance, he writes:

> If thou wilt say ... the sacrament of the blood is not to be received without the offering up and sacrificing thereof unto God the Father, both for the quick and the dead, and no man may make an oblation of Christ's blood unto God but a priest ... call you this, my masters, the *mysterium fidei*. Alas! alas! I fear me this is before God the *mysterium iniquitatis*. ... This kind of oblation standeth upon transubstantiation, its german cousin, and do grow both upon one ground. The Lord weed out of his vineyard shortly ... that bitter root.[2]

We have also the Reasons attached to the Order to take down the altars,[3] to which reference has already been made, for they are said to be of Ridley's composition, and at all events they were sent out by him to his clergy.

The other companions of Cranmer have written less, but the following short quotations are sufficient to prove that they were in agreement with their chief.

WILLIAM BARLOW, Bishop of St. David's, in answer to Henry VIII.'s *Questions* said:—'The oblation and sacrifice of Christ mentioned in the Mass is a *memorial* of Christ's only sacrifice upon the Cross once offered for ever'; with which corresponds his well-known statement at St. David's that a layman, if appointed by the King, 'without any mention of Orders, should be as good a Bishop as he is, or the best in England.'

NICHOLAS FERRAR.—'The adoration of the Sacrament with honour due to God, the reservation and carrying about of the same; the Mass to be a propitiatory sacrifice for the quick and the dead, or a work that pleaseth God—all those we believe and acknowledge to be the doctrine of antichrist.' This declaration was likewise signed by Hooper and Coverdale, two other

---

[1] *Works*, Parker Society's edition, pp. 12, 13.   [2] *Ibid.* p. 23.
[3] See above, p. 64.

Edwardine prelates, whose votes contributed to pass the Second Prayer Book through Parliament.[1]

GOODRICH, Bishop of Ely. Hooper in a letter to Bullinger had just said that Cranmer's 'sentiments concerning the Eucharist are pure and religious, and similar to yours in Switzerland,' and he adds : ' There are here six or seven Bishops who comprehend the doctrine of Christ as far as relates to the Lord's Supper with as much clearness and piety as one could desire.' And in another letter he gives their names—' the Bishops of Canterbury (Cranmer), Rochester (Ridley), Ely (Goodrich), St. David's (Ferrar), Lincoln (Holbeach), Bath (Barlow).'[2]

The above were Cranmer's episcopal associates. The following are the statements of divines belonging to Cranmer's party who assisted him in his liturgical reforms:

RICHARD COX, who became Bishop of Ely under Elizabeth : 'The oblation of the Sacrifice of the Mass consists of prayer, praise, thanksgiving, and commemoration of the Passion and Death of Christ.'[3]

JOHN TAYLOR, who became Bishop of Lincoln under Elizabeth : 'There is no oblation properly speaking [in the Mass], but some ancient doctors and the use of the Church call the receiving of the same with the circumstances then done an oblation, that is to say, a memorial and remembrance of Christ's most precious oblation upon the Cross.'[4]

MILES COVERDALE, already mentioned as having signed the declaration together with Ferrar and Hooper, deserves to be mentioned again as one who was conspicuous alike by the high opinion in which he was held by Cranmer and the reforming party, and by the violence of his invectives against the Mass. In 1550, that is, at the time when the First Prayer Book and Ordinal had just appeared, he was placed on a commission one among the duties of which was to punish those who did not duly administer the Sacraments according to the new Prayer Book. This Coverdale, in a book full of blasphemies against the Mass,[5] tells us that the Devil 'by giving his daughter

---

[1] Ap. Bradford, *Works*, p. 373, Parker's Society's Edition.
[2] *Original Letters* (First Portion), December 27, 1549, and February 5, 1550.
[3] *Stillingfleet MSS.*, loc. cit., fol. 11 and 18.   [4] *Ibid.* fol. 13.
[5] *On the Carrying of Christ's Cross, Works,* p. 267.

Idolatry . . . to the Pope and his shaven shorelings, they [the Pope and the Devil] **have** by this means in many years been begetting a daughter, which at length was delivered to destroy preaching, even the minion Missa, Mistress Missa, who danced daintily before the Herods of the world, and is the cause why John the Baptist and the preachers be put to prison and lose their heads.' This sentence is worthy of notice, for it bears witness that the retention or abolition of the Mass was **the** central cause of conflict between the adherents of the ancient faith and the party of so-called reform and revision; it shows us, in short, that a recent writer stated only the truth (though less than the whole truth) when he said that as between the pre-Reformation Church and the Anglican Church, which is the child of the Reformation, 'it is the Mass that matters, it is the Mass that makes the difference.'

VI

The Doctrine of the later Anglican Divines on the Holy Eucharistic as a Sacrifice (see p. 74).

It is thought by many that the great Anglican divines of the seventeenth and early eighteenth centuries taught the same doctrine on the Eucharistic Sacrifice in all essential points as the Catholic Church; and great stress has been laid on this supposed fact by High Church writers. It is admitted that the divines of the earlier period often surrendered too much, but it is suggested that this was only in virtue of the inevitable tendency of the human mind, which, when hotly engaged in revolt against one extreme, is prone to run too far into the other; and it is contended that, as soon as the Reformation had effectively established itself, the doctrine of the Anglican Church, in all its due balance and proportion, found expression in the writings of the seventeenth century divines. It is thus that Dr. Pusey speaks in Tract 81 of *Tracts for the Times*, the tract entitled *Testimony of Writers of the later English Church to the Doctrine of the Eucharistic Sacrifice*. 'The divines,' he says, 'of the sixteenth and seventeenth centuries had different offices: in the sixteenth we are to look for strong, broad statements of truths, which had been obscured by Popery, but often without the modifications which they require and receive from other portions of the Gospel; in the seventeenth we have the calmer, deeper statements of men to whom God had given peace from the first conflict . . . a well-proportioned and equable exhibition of the several parts of the Catholic faith.' Dr. Pusey in this tract gives passages from a *catena* of sixteenth, seventeenth, and eighteenth century divines who undoubtedly maintain that the Eucharist is a sacrifice, and it is not unnatural that the High Churchmen should attach importance to the testimony. Still, on inspection, it will be found that these writers do not really go beyond the doctrine of Archbishop Cranmer, as exhibited in the passages quoted in the Letter, or the summaries likewise there quoted of Waterland and Newman—in other words, do not go beyond a sacrifice in which the thing offered is the prayer and praise, the alms-deeds and self-oblation of the people, or, at most, the bread and wine as representative symbols of our Lord's Body and Blood. That this is the case may be seen from the following list of quotations, most of which are taken from Dr. Pusey's *catena*. The list begins with Guest, whose opinions are set forth at somewhat greater length on account of the part he took in revising Article XXVIII. in the reign of Elizabeth.

GUEST.—Edmund Guest was a prominent Protestant ecclesiastic in the early days of Elizabeth, by whom he was appointed, first, Archdeacon of Canterbury and then Bishop of Rochester. He was on the Commission appointed in 1559 for the revision, with a view to its reintroduction, of the Prayer Book of Edward VI.

In King Edward's reign he published a *Treatise against Privie Mass*, in which the following passage occurs:

The privy mass worshippers hold opinion that Christ ought of congruence to be honoured and prayed after the consecration as being in the priest's hands for that He is then there both God and man, and so there no less honourable and prayable than in heaven. But this argumentation is nothing dialectical or formal. For that the presence of Christ in a place importeth not the honour and praying of Him in the said place. . . Christ is present in each assembly assembled faithfully in His name, yet notwithstanding no man doth honour and pray unto Him as resyant [i.e. resident] in the religious assembly but in heaven alone. Is He not as God each where and consequently at the mass? Howbeit no man judgeth Him there to be worshipped and called upon if His body were thence absented. The experience whereof is plain in that part of the mass that foregoeth the consecration. Why then should His bodily presence enforce us to honour and solicit Him in the said mass? For His bodily presence is not honourable nor prayable merely of itself but in respect of His Godhead personally allied and coupled therewith. Christ *both God and Man* with His Father and the Holy Ghost is *present at the Baptism* of faithful infants. When they become embodied and incorporate thereto it is to wete when they eat His Body and drink His Blood *as really as* we do at His Supper. Howbeit no man worshippeth His body as present at Baptism *there no less presented* than at His Supper, either else His Godhead, either for his [i.e. its] own or for the presence of His Body.[1]

From this passage we see that the kind of Real Presence in which Guest believed was one which could be found as truly and fully in Baptism as in the Holy Eucharist, and we learn also that his position was that of the Ubiquitarians, who believed in the omnipresence of the Sacred Humanity. Another passage from the same treatise shows that, consistently with these two points of belief, he declined to attach any efficacy to the act of consecration.

Consecration (he says) is that parcel of the mass where the priest presumeth to consecrate and hallow Christ's Body and Blood. The which, as it is an attempt too unreasonable and unable, so passing wicked presumptuous and detestable, for how can it be possible that Christ's Body, which cannot be holier and perfecter than already it is, should or might be consecrated of the priest? ... These words 'Take and eat' in these words of institution of the Lord's Supper, 'Take, eat, this is my Body,' be no words of making of the Lord's Body, but of presenting and exhibiting the same to the receivers of the Supper of the Lord. So that it is full open that the priest can neither consecrate Christ's Body, neither make it. Howbeit this is always grantable. The minister both consecrateth and maketh, though not Christ's Body, yet the hallowed bread and wine, the sacraments exhibitive of the same.[2]

The *Treatise on the Privie Mass* was written in 1548. In 1559 Guest, as one of the commissioners for revision, was called upon to return answers to certain questions propounded by Cecil. These answers show that the intervening period had effected no change in his views on the Eucharist.

[1] *Life and Character of Bishop Guest.* By H. G. Dugdale, p. 116.   [2] *Ibid.*, p. 78.

One of these questions was, 'Whether in the celebration of Holy Communion priests should not use a cope besides a surplice.' Guest answers in the negative:

> Because it is thought sufficient to use but a surplice in baptising, reading, preaching, and praying, therefore it is enough also for the celebrating of the Communion. For if we should use another garment herein, it should seem to teach us that higher and better things be given by it than be given by the other service [Baptism], which we must not believe. For in Baptism we put on Christ, in the word we eat and drink Christ, as Jerome and Gregory write, and Augustine saith the word is as precious as this sacrament, saying 'he sinneth as much which negligently heareth the word as he which willingly letteth Christ's Body to fall on the ground,' and Chrysostom saith, 'he which is not fit to receive is not fit to pray' which were not true if prayer were not of as much importance as Holy Communion.[1]

Another question was, 'Whether the Prayer of consecration in the First Communion Book [*i.e.* the service in the First Prayer Book of Edward VI.] should be left out. The prayer in question is the prayer which is cited as of importance in the *Responsio*, 'Hear, O merciful Father, we beseech Thee, and with Thy Holy Spirit and word vouchsafe to bl + ess and sanc + tify these Thy gifts and creatures of bread and wine, that they may be unto us the Body and Blood of Thy most dearly-beloved Son, Jesus Christ, who on the same night that He was betrayed, &c.' In the Second Prayer Book of Edward VI. this prayer was removed, in deference to the protests of Bucer and others, and in place of it was substituted the following: 'Grant that we, receiving these Thy creatures of bread and wine, according to Thy Son our Saviour Jesus Christ's holy institution, in remembrance of His death and passion, may be partakers of His Body and Blood, who in the same night, &c.' Cecil's question was whether the earlier prayer should continue to be left out and give place to the latter.

Guest's answer is a decided 'Yes,' which he justifies in these terms:

> This prayer is to be disliked for two causes: the first because it is taken to be so needful for the consecration that the consecration is not thought to be without it, which is not true; ... the second cause is, for

---

[1] *Life and Character of Bishop Guest*, p. 145.

it prayeth that the bread and wine may be Christ's Body and Blood, which maketh for the popish transubstantiation, which is a doctrine that hath caused much idolatry.[1]

JEWELL, in his *Defence of the Apology*, says:

Have we no external sacrifice, say you? I beseech you, what sacrifice did Christ or His apostles ever command that we have refused? . . . We have the sacrifice of prayer, the sacrifice of alms-deeds, the sacrifice of praise, the sacrifice of thanksgiving, and the sacrifice of the Death of Christ. We are taught to present our bodies as a pure, and a holy, and a well-pleasing sacrifice unto God, and to offer unto Him the burning sacrifices of our lips. These (saith St. Paul) are the sacrifices wherewith God is pleased. These be the sacrifices of the Church of God. Whoever hath these we cannot say he is void of sacrifice. . . . You **will** say, Ye offer not up Christ really unto God His Father. No, **Mr. Harding**; neither we nor you can so offer **Him, nor** did Christ ever **give** you commission to **offer up such a sacrifice. And this it** is wherewith you so beguile the simple.[2]

BISHOP BILSON, in his *Subjection and Rebellion*, says:

The Fathers with one consent call not your private Mass, that they never knew, but the Lord's Supper a sacrifice, which we both willingly grant and openly teach. . . . For there, besides the sacrifices of praise and thanksgiving, which we must then offer to God for our redemption and other His graces . . . besides the dedication of **our** souls and bodies to be a reasonable, quick, and holy sacrifice to serve and please Him; besides the contributions and alms . . . a sacrifice no doubt very **acceptable to** God; I say besides these three sundry sorts of offerings **incident to the** Lord's table, the very supper itself is a public memorial **of that great and** dreadful sacrifice, I mean of the death and blood-shedding of our Saviour. . . . This oblation *of bread and wine*, for a thanksgiving to God, and a memorial **of His** Son's death, was so confessed and undoubted a truth in **the Church of Christ till** your schoolmen began to wrest both Scriptures and Fathers. . . .[3]

HOOKER, in his *Ecclesiastical Polity*, says:

No side denieth but that the **soul** of man is the receptacle of Christ's **presence** [in the Eucharist] . . . nor doth anything rest doubtful but this, whether when the Sacrament is administered Christ be whole **within the man only, or else** His **Body and Blood be** also externally **seated in the** very consecrated **elements themselves**; which opinion they **that** defend are driven either to *consubstantiate* **and** incorporate Christ with the elements sacramental, or to *transubstantiate* and change their

---

[1] *Life and Character of Bishop Guest*, p. 148.
[2] P. ii. p. 336. Parker Society's edition.   [3] P. 688. Edition of 1585.

substance into His. . . . Is there anything more expedite, clear, and easy than that, as Christ is termed our life, so the parts of this Sacrament are His Body and Blood, for that they are so to us who receiving them receive that by them which they are termed? The bread and cup are His Body and Blood, because they are the causes instrumental upon the receipt whereof the participation of His Body and Blood ensueth. For that which produceth any certain effect is not vainly nor improperly said to be that very effect whereunto it tendeth. . . . The real presence of Christ's Body and Blood **is not therefore to** be sought for in the Sacrament, but in the worthy receiver **of the** sacrament. . . . Seeing that sacrifice is now no part of the Church's ministry, how should the name of Priesthood be **thereunto rightly applied?** . . . The Fathers of the Church of Christ . . . call usually the ministry of the Gospel Priesthood in regard of **that** which the Gospel hath proportionable to ancient sacrifice, namely, **the** Communion of the blessed Body **and** Blood of Christ, although it **have** properly now **no** sacrifice.[1]

OVERALL.—In Dr. Pusey's *catena* Overall figures largely, the doctrine ascribed to him being taken from 'notes written in an interleaved Common Prayer Book printed in the year 1619, supposed to be made from the collections of Bishop Overall by a friend or chaplain of his.'[2] But it is now known that the notes are by Cosin, being sometimes Cosin's own, sometimes extracts from the works of others which, in his judgment, throw light on the text of the Prayer Book. Occasionally he cites some saying or practice of Overall's, whose chaplain he had formerly been.[3] As these notes do not give Overall's opinion on any point of consequence, and his opinion is not otherwise ascertainable, his name must be passed over. Cosin's opinions will be cited presently.

ANDREWES, who is described by a recent Anglican historian as 'standing out above all his compeers as the typical representative of the English Church,' is most evasive in his references to the Real Objective Presence and the Eucharistic Sacrifice. It is clear, however, that he held no higher doctrine in regard to it than the divines already quoted, as may be seen from his reply to Cardinal Du Perron. Cardinal Du Perron had stated the doctrine of the primitive Church, with plentiful references to the Fathers. As regards the Real Presence he had said:

[1] Bk. V. chap. lxvii. n. 2, 6; chap. lxxviii. n. 2. Edition of 1841.
[2] See *Additional Notes on The Common Prayer* in Nicholl's Commentary.
[3] See Cosin's *Works*, vol. v. Preface, *Library of Anglo-Catholic Theology*.

The Catholic Church at the time of St. Augustine and of the first four Councils [was] a Church which believed in the true and real presence and oral eating of the Body of Christ in the Sacrament, under and in the sacramental species . . . a Church which as such adored the Eucharist, not only with interior thoughts and devotions, but with external gestures and adorations, as containing really and substantially the true and real Body of Christ: for I do not want to speak of Transubstantiation at present, as I am reserving that for a separate treatise.[1] .

Andrewes devotes five pages to meeting this statement, pages which surely no one can regard as other than quibbling, and in which the only unambiguous statement made is that the Fathers quoted by Du Perron for Eucharistic adoration must be held to mean veneration, not adoration, and that 'we by the grace of God hold the Sacrament to be venerable, and with all due respect to be handled and received,' but that '*the symbols so abiding*, it is easily known that no Divine adoration can be given to them.'[2]

As regards the Eucharistic Sacrifice Du Perron had said:

The primitive Church was a Church which believed in a true, full, and entire sacrifice, succeeding of itself alone to all the sacrifices of the law; the new oblation of the New Testament, the external worship of adoration among the Christians; and not only a Eucharistic sacrifice, but also a propitiatory sacrifice, by the application of that of the Cross; and which [Church] in this quality offered it both for communicants and non-communicants, for the living and for the dead.[3]

Du Perron was assuming that the Anglican Church had not such a sacrifice, and it will be noticed that Andrewes, in his reply, says indeed that his Church does believe the Eucharist to be a sacrifice, but evades altogether the question of its nature, and after the first clause speaks only of the Sacrifice of the Cross.

1. The Eucharist ever was and by us is considered both as a sacrament and as a sacrifice. 2. A sacrifice is proper and applicable only to Divine worship. 3. The sacrifice of Christ's death did succeed to the sacrifices of the Old Testament. 4. The sacrifice of Christ's death is available for present, absent, living, dead (yea, for them that are unborn). 5. When we say 'dead' we mean it is available for the Apostles, Martyrs, Confessors, and all (because we are members of one body). These no

---

[1] See Andrewes' *Works, Answers to Card. Perron*, p. 7, *Library of Anglo-Catholic Theology*.

[2] *Ibid.* pp. 16, 17.   [3] *Ibid.* p. 8.

man will deny. 6. In a word, we hold with St. Augustine in the very same chapter which the Cardinal citeth, that 'the flesh and blood of this sacrifice before the coming of Christ was promised through victims of similitude; in the Passion of Christ was given through the very truth; and after the ascension through the sacrament of memorial.' [1]

LAUD, in his Conference with Fisher says:

As Christ offered up Himself once for all a full and all-sufficient sacrifice for the sin of the whole world, so did He institute and command a memory of this sacrifice in a sacrament, even till His coming again. For at and in the Eucharist we offer to God three sacrifices. One by the priest only; that's the commemorative sacrifice of Christ's death represented in bread broken and wine poured out. Another by the priest and people jointly; and that is the sacrifice of praise and thanksgiving for all the benefits and graces we receive by the precious death of Christ. The third by every particular man for himself only; and that is the sacrifice of every man's body and soul to serve Him in both all the rest of his life for this blessing thus bestowed upon him.[2]

And in his *History of his Troubles* he says:

Bellarmine . . . doth well . . . if (he) mean no more by the oblation of the Body and Blood of Christ than a commemoration and a representation of that great sacrifice offered by Christ Himself. . . . But if Bellarmine go further than this, and by the oblation of the Body and Blood of Christ, mean that the priest offers up that which Christ Himself did, and not a commemoration of it only, he is erroneous in that, and can never make it good.[3]

MEDE, as the writer of a work entitled *The Christian Sacrifice*, was regarded by subsequent Anglican divines as a special authority on the subject. He sums up his doctrine in six propositions:

1. This Christian service is an oblation, and expressed under that notion by the utmost antiquity.

2. It is an oblation of thanksgiving and prayer.

3. An oblation through Jesus Christ commemorated in the creatures of bread and wine.

4. This commemoration of Christ, according to the style of the ancient Church, is also a sacrifice.

---

[1] Andrewes' *Works, Answers to Card. Perron*, p. 19.

[2] *Conference with Fisher*, Laud's *Works*, ii. 339, *Library of Anglo-Catholic Theology*.

[3] *History of his Troubles*, Laud's *Works*, iv. 358, *Library of Anglo-Catholic Theology*.

5. The Body and Blood of Christ, in this mystical service, was made of bread and wine, which had first been offered unto God, to agnize [*i.e.* 'to acknowledge'] Him the Lord of the creature.

6. This sacrifice was placed in commemoration only of Christ's sacrifice upon the Cross, and not in a real offering of His Body and Blood anew.[1]

The only point here which may seem doubtful is the **fifth**, but a little lower down in the same volume he explains: 'They [the ancient Church] first offered the bread and wine unto God to agnize Him the Lord of the creature, and then received them again from Him in a banquet as the symbols of the Body and Blood of His Son.'[2] And lower down still: 'Well, then, Christ is offered in this sacred Supper, not hypostatically [*i.e.* personally] as the Papists would have Him (for so He was but once offered), but commemoratively only; that is, by this sacred rite of bread and wine we present and inculcate His Blessed **Passion** to His Father, **or** put Him **in mind** thereof **by** setting **the monuments** thereof before Him.'[3]

COSIN, in his Notes in the interleaved Prayer-Book of 1636, says:

By the ancients and by us the celebration of this sacrament is called a sacrifice, yea, a true sacrifice in the manner we have explained it in. First, because it is a sensible rite, supplying the place of sensible things. Secondly, because, when it is celebrated, those things are wont to be offered, which were used in sacrifices, or at least went to the use of the ministers of the Church, or the poor, which in Scripture language are called 'sacrifices acceptable to God.' Thirdly, because therein thanks are given to God, and prayers are poured out which in Scripture are styled by the name of sacrifice. Fourthly, **because by** these prayers the Passion, Death, and Merits of Christ are offered **up to God** the Father by commemoration and representation.[4]

Cosin's doctrine on the Real Presence may also be gathered from his pronouncements, that 'a sacramental expression doth without any inconvenience give to the sign the name of the thing signified,' and 'hence . . . the bread is **as** clearly or positively

---

[1] *The Christian Sacrifice*, sect. 3, p. 483. Edition of **1648**.
[2] *Ibid.* p. 519.   [3] *Ibid.* p. **522**.
[4] **Note on words** *Offer unto Thee any* **sacrifice**. The note is taken from Calixtus, the Lutheran (*De Sacr. Christi*, p. xciii), but Cosin inserted it because it expressed his own meaning.

called by the apostle the Communion of the Body of Christ';[1] and that 'none of the Protestant Churches doubt of the real (*i.e.* the true, not imaginary) presence of Christ's Body and Blood in the Sacrament,'[2] a statement which he defends by citations from the Prayer Book of his own Church, the Augsburg Confession, the Wittenberg Confession, the Bohemian Confession, the Polish Agreement, the Strasburg Confession, the French (Protestant) Confession, and the Helvetic Confession, and likewise by a citation from Calvin. A Real Presence which was accepted by all these Protestant formularies is clearly not the kind of Real Presence in which the Catholic Church believes; and that it was a presence which in Cosin's mind was altogether dissociated even from the bread and wine as soon as the Communion Service was over, may be gathered from his marginal note, in the interleaved Prayer Book of 1638, to the words 'if any of the bread and wine remain':

> Yet, if for lack of care they consecrate more than they distribute, why may not the curates have it for their own use, as well as be given to the children (*Conc. Matisc.* c. 2) or be burnt in the fire (Isych. in Leon.); for though the bread and wine remain, yet after the consecration, the Sacrament of the Body and Blood of Christ do not remain longer than the holy action itself remains for which the bread and wine was hallowed; and which, being ended, return to their former use again.[3]

HAMMOND puts to himself the question, 'What is the full importance of that which follows in the latter part of the answer [of the Church Catechism] that the Body and Blood of Christ are verily and indeed taken and received by the faithful in the Lord's Supper?' He replies:

> It is this that . . . as truly as the Bishop or Presbyter gives me the sacramental bread and wine, so truly doth God in heaven bestow upon me on earth the Body and Blood of Christ, *i.e.* the crucified Saviour; not by local motion, but by real communication not to our teeth, but to our souls, and consequently exhibits or makes over or reaches out unto us the benefits thereof.[4]

With these views of the Real Presence it was only open to him to hold a sacrifice of bare commemoration, which, accord-

---

[1] *History of Transubstantiation*, Chap. I, n. 4, iv. 156, *Library of Anglo-Catholic Theology*.
[2] *Ibid.* Chap. II. n. 1, p. 157.   [3] *Ibid.* p. 356.
[4] *Practical Catechism, Works*, i. 396, *Library of Anglo-Catholic Theology*.

ingly, he does a little higher up in the same Catechism: 'The breaking and eating of the bread is a communication of the Body of Christ—a sacrifice commemorative of Christ's offering up His Body for us, and making us partakers, or communicating to us the benefits of that bread of life, strengthening and giving us grace.'

THORNDIKE stands out among the Caroline divines as the one who understood most accurately the Catholic doctrine of the Eucharist, and who tried to judge it in the spirit of fairness. His own doctrine, however, in spite of some phrases which savour of a doctrine of impanation, was substantially the same with that of the rest. In his Epilogue he finds four modes of sacrifice in the Eucharist, which he thus allocates briefly in his marginal notes: (1) 'in the oblation of the elements before their consecration'; (2) 'in the offering of prayer for all estates of men'; (3) 'in regard of the consecration'; (4) 'in the oblation to God of the bodies and souls of the receivers.' Here the only doubt which would arise would be as to the third of these modes, although the bare fact that he should think the three others to be sufficiently commensurable with it shows already that he cannot be thinking of the sacrifice founded in a Real Objective Presence. Nor does he. A little lower down he writes thus:[1]

What then shall we say when the name of Christ's Body and Blood is attributed to the bread and wine of the Eucharist, but that God would have us understand a supernatural conjunction and union between the Body and Blood of Christ and the said bread and wine, whereby they become as truly the instrument for conveying God's Spirit to them who receive as they ought as the same Spirit was always in His natural Body and Blood.

JEREMY TAYLOR, in his treatise *Of the Real Presence of Christ in the Holy Sacrament*, says:

The doctrine of the Church of England, and generally of the Protestants in this article, is that after the minister of the holy mysteries hath rightly prayed, and blessed or consecrated the bread and the wine, the symbols become changed into the Body and Blood of Christ, after a sacramental, that is, a spiritual real manner; so that all that

---

[1] *Epilogue*, P. III. *Laws of God*. Works, tom. iv. pp. 106 &c. *Library of Anglo-Catholic Theology.*

worthily communicate do by faith receive Christ really, effectually, to all the purposes of His passion: the wicked receive not Christ, but the bare symbols only: but yet to their hurt, because the offer of Christ is rejected, and they pollute the blood of the covenant by using it as an unholy thing. The result of which doctrine is this: it is bread, and it is Christ's Body. It is bread in substance, Christ in the sacrament: and Christ is as really given to all that are truly disposed as the symbols are ... and Christ does as really nourish and sanctify the soul as the elements do the body. *It is here as in the other sacrament*; for as there natural water becomes the laver of regeneration; so here bread and wine become the Body and Blood of Christ; but there and here too the first substance is changed by grace, but remains the same in nature.[1]

And in the previous page he had said:

Our word of 'spiritual presence' is particular in nothing, but that it excludes the corporal and natural manner; or say it is not this, but it is to be understood figuratively, that is, not naturally, but to the purposes and in the manner of the spirit and spiritual things, which how they operate or are effected, we know no more than we know how a cherub sings or thinks.... Christ is present spiritually, that is by effect and blessing; which, in true speaking, is *rather the consequent* of His presence *than the formality*.

BULL, in his *Corruptions of the Church of Rome*, in answer to the Bishop of Meaux' queries, quotes the article in the Creed of Pius IV. which professes that 'in the Mass is offered to God a true, proper, and propitiatory sacrifice for the living and the dead'; that 'in the most Holy Eucharist there is truly, really, and substantially the Body and Blood, together with the Soul and Divinity of Our Lord Jesus Christ; and that there is wrought a conversion of the whole substance ... which conversion the Catholic Church calls Transubstantiation.' In his comment he condemns each of these three assertions separately, leaving no pretext to anyone who might suggest that he repudiated only Transubstantiation. He says, as regards the first two points:[2] ...

This proposition [that 'in the Mass there is offered to God a true, proper, and propitiatory sacrifice for the living and the dead'] having that other of the 'substantial presence of the Body and Blood of Christ in the Eucharist' immediately annexed to it, the meaning must necessarily be this, that in the Eucharist the very Body and Blood of Christ

---

[1] *Works*, ix. 425. Edition of 1822. [2] Pp. 22 &c. Edition of 1813.

are again offered up to God as a propitiatory sacrifice for the sins of men, which is an impious proposition, derogatory to the one full satisfaction of Christ made by His death on the Cross. . . . It is true the Eucharist is frequently called by the ancient Fathers προσφορά, θυσία, an 'oblation,' a 'sacrifice.' But it is to be remembered that they say also it is θυσία λογική καὶ ἀναίμακτος, a 'reasonable **sacrifice**,' a 'sacrifice without blood,' which how **can** it be said to **be if** therein the **very Blood of** Christ were offered up to God?

HICKES, in his *Christian Priesthood Asserted*, says:

I hope I have said enough to make it appear **that** all the ancient Churches believed **bread and** wine **to** be the **proper** subject matter of the Christian **oblation in the Holy Eucharist, or the** sensible things which they **really offered, and believed** ought **to be really** offered to God, in that holy service for **the sacrificial feast.** . . . Were I to define the Eucharistical Sacrifice, it should be in these forms. The Eucharistical Sacrifice is *an oblation of bread and wine*, instituted by Jesus Christ, to represent and commemorate His sacrifice upon the Cross.[1]

JOHNSON begins his treatise on the *Propitiatory Oblation in the Holy Eucharist* with an apology for suppressing his name. **He says** he **has** suppressed it because of the unpopularity of the **doctrine he is about** to advocate, and **then at** once he proceeds **to** deprecate **the** charge of Popery by distinguishing between the Catholic sacrifice and that of the English High Church divines.

1. **The** Papists hold that in the Sacrifice of the Mass the whole Christ, God and Man, **is** offered up hypostatically to **the** Father in the Holy Eucharist, and is to be worshipped thus by **men** under the species of bread **and wine.** This doctrine is utterly renounced by all Protestants— **by those who** assert the Eucharistic **Sacrifice as well as those who deny it.**

2. The Papists assert the substantial presence of Christ's **Body** and Blood, under the species of bread and wine in the Holy Eucharist, and that the Sacrifices of the Cross and of the Altar are substantially the same. But **this is** peremptorily denied by those who declare for the oblation of **the Eucharist in the** Church of England. . . .

On the other side it will appear:
1. That not the divinity and human soul of Christ Jesus, but His Body and Blood only are offered in the Eucharist.
2. That not His substantial, but sacramental Body and Blood are there offered.

---

[1] Prefatory Account to the 3rd Edition.

And in his *Unbloody Sacrifice* he says:

Though the ancients believed the bread and wine in the Eucharist to be the Body and Blood; yet they did not believe that they were the natural or substantial Body and Blood, but that they were so *in a spiritual manner, in power and effect*. So that the bread and wine are not the Body and Blood in themselves considered, nor merely by their resembling or representing the Body and Blood, but by the invisible power of the Spirit, by which the sacramental Body and Blood are made as powerful and effectual for the ends of religion as the natural body and blood itself could be if it was present. And it is on this account that it is called Christ's spiritual and mysterious Body, as being what it is by [? to] the inward not the outward eye: by our faith, our minds and spirits, not our senses. And this ... is a full answer to the objections above mentioned: for though bread and wine, abstractedly considered, are indeed weak elements; yet when enriched with the special presence, and invisible operations of the Spirit, they are very efficacious and beneficial.[1]

Passages to the same effect might without difficulty be extracted from the works of other Anglican divines, but it would be hard to collect any, before the middle of the present century, which assert the Real Objective Presence and literal sacrifice in the sense of the Catholic Church. On the other hand, a similar series of Anglican divines could be cited who vehemently protested against even the mild sacrificial doctrine of the above passages. Hickes, for instance, and Johnson complain much of the charges of Popery brought against them for advocating it. But their accusers were certainly absurd in this, for when this High Church doctrine is analysed it appears at once that it was not only not Popery, but that, except for the phraseology used in expounding it, it was essentially the same as the Low Church doctrine of the accusers themselves. There is, in fact, no mean between the Catholic doctrine of a Real Objective Presence and the Zwinglian doctrine of pure symbols. The intermediate doctrines, fiercely though they have been claimed as distinctive of the different parties and sects, are but the Zwinglian doctrine enveloped in a mist of words void of meaning. So, at least, it seems; but in any case the conclusion stands that the Catholic doctrine of the Presence and Sacrifice is essentially different from the sacrificial doctrine of the great Anglican divines.

[1] *Unbloody Sacrifice*, I. 266, Lib. A.-C. Theol.

VII

The Synod of Bethlehem **on the** *Holy Eucharist* (see p. 82).

What is so noticeable and puzzling about the great Anglican divines, when they undertake to expound to us their doctrine on the Holy Eucharist as a sacrament and a sacrifice, is the vague and deceptive character of their language. The passages selected for quotation in the last Appendix are passages from which it seems possible to arrive at certainty about the meaning of the writers. But if one opens Dr. Pusey's *Tract* 81, or, still better, the treatises themselves of these divines, one may read page after page without being able to ascertain whether the writers believe in a Real Objective Presence or not. This strange phenomenon of itself alone suggests an argument worthy of consideration. If, as is nowadays claimed for them, these Anglican divines really held (substantially) the same doctrine of the Real Presence and the Sacrifice of the Mass as the Catholic Church holds, why is it that, capable men as they undoubtedly were, they should have been, one and all, so unable to expound their meaning in language of clear and unmistakable character? Why, for instance, could they not have spoken with the same distinctness as the Synod of Bethlehem of 1672, whose Seventeenth Article is here transcribed that it may be seen how completely the doctrine on the Eucharist of the great Eastern Churches separated from the Holy See is identical with that of the Catholic Church?

By way of previous explanation, it is enough to say that, according to Dr. Mason Neale, an unsuspected witness, St. John Damascene's treatise, *De Fide Orthodoxa*, was for long 'the great storehouse of Eastern Orthodoxy, holding in the East a place similar to that of the *Sentences* in the West.' No other authorised doctrinal exposition was made by these Churches till the seventeenth century. Then came several occasioned by the invasion of Calvinistic propagandism. Prominent among these later doctrinal expositions are the Eighteen Articles of the Synod of Bethlehem in 1672, adopted formally, with one qualification not now concerning us, by the Russian Synod of 1838.

DOCTRINE OF THE SYNOD OF BETHLEHEM

The portion of these articles bearing on the question in hand is given in Dr. Mason Neale's translation from the Russian text of 1838, the variants of Provost Maltzew's German translation from the same and those of the Greek original of 1672 being given in brackets.

'We believe that the most holy Mystery of the Divine Eucharist, which we have reckoned above as the fourth in order, is that Mystery which the Lord instituted on that night in which He delivered up Himself for the life of the world. For when He had taken bread and blessed it, He gave it to His disciples and apostles, saying, Take, Eat: this is My Body. And when He had taken the cup, He gave thanks and said, Drink ye all of it: this is My Blood which is shed for you for the remission of sins. We believe that, in the celebration of this Mystery, our Lord Jesus Christ is present, not in a figurative or imaginary manner, nor by any excellency of grace, as in the other Mysteries, nor by a bare presence, as some Fathers have said of Baptism, nor by impanation, nor by the substantial [M. 'so that there is a hypostatical'] union of the Divinity of the Word with the bread which is set upon the Altar, as the Lutherans ignorantly and wretchedly [M. 'unworthily'] explain it [Greek 'think'], but verily and indeed; so that after the consecration of the bread and wine, the bread is changed, transubstantiated, transmuted, transformed, into the very true Body and Blood of our Lord, which was born in Bethlehem of the most pure Virgin, baptized in the river Jordan, suffered, was buried, rose again, ascended into heaven, sitteth on the right hand of the Father, shall come again in the clouds of heaven; and the wine is transubstantiated into the very true Blood of the Lord, which was shed for the life of the world when He suffered upon the Cross.

'Further, we believe that, after the consecration of the bread and wine, the very bread and wine no longer remain [Greek, 'the substance of the bread and wine no longer remains,' M. 'the substance of the bread and wine no longer remains'], but the very Body and Blood of our Lord, under the appearance and form of bread and wine [the Greek adds, 'that is to say, under the accidents of the bread']. Further, we believe that this most pure Body and Blood of our Lord is distributed, and enters into the mouth and stomach of the communicants, whether they be godly or wicked. Only that to the godly they procure remission of sins and eternal life, while to the ungodly they prepare condemnation and eternal torments. . . .

'Further, we believe that the Body and Blood of the Lord ought to be especially honoured and worshipped with Divine worship. For the worship which we are bound to pay to our Lord Jesus Christ Himself we are bound also to pay to the Body and Blood of the Lord [M. 'for the worship which we give to the Lord (or the Holy Trinity) is one and the same with that we give to the Body and Blood of the Lord '].

'Further, we believe that this is a true and propitiatory sacrifice for all the [M. 'the good'] quick and dead [M. 'and for the good of all'] as is expressly contained in the prayers belonging to this Mystery which have been delivered by the Apostles to the Church, according as they had received commandment of the Lord [for the salvation of all].

'Further, we believe that this sacrifice, as well before it has been administered to anyone immediately after its consecration as after it has been received—that is, that which is kept in the holy vessels for the purpose of giving Communion to the dying— is the true Body of the Lord, and differing in no respect from His Body; so that before it is received after consecration, during reception, and after reception, it still remains the true Body of the Lord. Further, when we use the word transubstantiation ($\mu\varepsilon\tau o\upsilon\sigma\iota\omega\sigma\iota s$), we by no means think it explains the mode in which the bread and wine are converted into the Body and Blood of the Lord, for this is altogether incomprehensible, and impossible for anyone to understand, but God alone; and the attempt to understand it can only be the result of irreverence and impiety; but we mean that the bread and wine after the consecration are changed into the Body and Blood of the Lord, not figuratively or symbolically, nor by any extraordinary grace attached to them, nor by the communication or descent of the divinity alone of the Only Begotten Son, nor is any accidental property of the bread and wine converted into any accidental property of the Body and Blood of Christ by any kind of change or mixture; but, as has been said above, the bread becomes ($\gamma i\nu\varepsilon\tau a\iota$) verily, and indeed, and substantially the very true Body of the Lord, and the wine the very Blood of the Lord.'[1]

Whether in this declaration Dr. Neale's or Provost Maltzew's, the Russian or the Greek, variants are to be preferred in the few cases where they are found, is of no consequence for the purpose now in hand. Provost Maltzew's authority, as that of a distinguished theologian of the Russian Church, necessarily stands higher than Dr. Neale's, and his readings, whilst they tend to show that any differences between the Greek and the Russian text are unessential, recommend themselves also as being more theologically correct. Still the only question the variants can affect is the question whether or not these Eastern Churches hold the doctrine of Transubstantiation, Provost Maltzew's versions representing that they do, and Dr. Neale's somewhat slurring this point over. As regards the Real Objective Presence, the true Propitiatory Sacrifice, and the true Priesthood, the doctrines on which the question of a valid Ordinal turns, the teaching of this Synod of Bethlehem, whatever view we take of the few variants, is identical with that of the Holy See and in sharp contrast with that of the great Anglican divines, as exhibited in the quotations of Appendix VI.

Nor can the authority of this Synod with the Russian Church be denied, for on this point Provost Maltzew, in a work published last summer,[2] and dedicated to M. Pobedonoszew, the Procurator of the Holy Synod, speaks as follows:

Two Anglican theologians, Professor Collins and Mr. Birkbeck, in a *brochure* published in London in 1897, and entitled *Cardinal Vaughan and the Russian Church*, have put forward the theory that the Russian Church does not accept the doctrine expressed in the original Greek text of the Decrees of the Orthodox Fathers [*i.e.* in the Synod of Bethlehem], according to which the substance (οὐσία) of the Bread and Wine is changed into the substance of the Body and Blood of Christ whilst the accidents (τὰ βεβηκότα) of the Bread remain. . . . But it is not permissible for a

---

[1] For Dr. Neale's translation see his *History of the Eastern Church*, Gen. Introd. vol. ii. p. 1173; for Provost Maltzew's, see his *Liturgien der Orthodox-Katholischen Kirche*, p. 219; and for the Greek text Kimmel's *Mon. Fid. Eccl. Orient.* i. p. 458.

[2] *Bitt-, Dank- und Weihe-Gottesdienste der Orthodox-Katholischen Kirche des Morgenlandes*, p. ci.

particular Church, such as **the** Russian Church, to depart in any point whatsoever, whether essential or trifling, from the **doctrine** which is contained in the official Confessions of the whole Orthodox Eastern Church, **the** original Greek text of which [Confessions] is sanctioned by the authority of the Most Holy **Patriarchs.** The doctrines therein contained are without **exception** unchangeable *dogmas* of the infallible *magisterium* of the **Holy** Church—of that *magisterium* which is inspired by the Holy Ghost **and** exercised by the divinely instituted hierarchy, and of that Church **which** can neither deceive nor be deceived. In regard **to** all these dogmas **there** prevails among all the particular Orthodox Churches an *absolute agreement*, and any departure, however slight, from these Confessions— the *Confessio Orthodoxa* [of 1643], the *Decrees of the Orthodox Patriarchs* [of Bethlehem **in** 1672], and the *Longer Christian Catechism of the Orthodox Catholic **Eastern** Church* [of 1838]—must be regarded **as** nothing less **than** heresy.'

But **this typical** Russian theologian in the same recent work goes further still. **He not** only claims an unimpeachable authority **for** a doctrinal statement in entire agreement with the teaching **of** the *Apostolicæ Curæ*; he also pronounces on the corresponding teaching of **the** Anglican Communion exactly the same judgment as Leo **XIII.** Considering **the** question **of** possible reunion between his **own** Church and other Christian Communions he lays down the principle that his Church can regard reunion **as possible** between itself **and** all such other Christian Churches **as have** preserved the *successio apostolica*, provided only that they be ready to renounce every doctrine in which they at present differ **from** it. He then enumerates the Churches which he considers **to have** retained the *successio apostolica*, and they **are** the '**Oriental Churches (as,** for example, the Ethiopian, the Coptic, **the Syrian, the** Armenian, &c.) and the Roman,' to which list of ancient **Churches** he presently adds, as possibly falling in the same category, the ' Old Catholics ' of **Germany.** Next, passing to the Protestant Communions, he excludes them all from his list, as not possessing the *successio apostolica*, and goes **on to** speak of the Anglican Communion as follows :

> In this respect the Anglican **Church (High** Church) is no exception [among the Communions, which originated **in** the ' Reformation ']. As we have **already in another** place had occasion to explain [*i.e.* in his *Dogmat. Erörterungen*, pp. 36-40], it is equally destitute of the *successio apostolica*, **the** ordination of priests according to the teaching of this Church **not being regarded** as a sacrament, and the most essential

functions of the priesthood, by reason of its anomalous doctrine on the Eucharist, not being exercised within its fold. And this is what the present Pope, in spite of his enthusiasm for the union of the Churches, has found himself constrained to declare, therein agreeing with a declaration of the Old Catholic Bishops of Holland in 1894.[1]

Provost Maltzew adds on behalf of his Communion words which exactly express the attitude of the Catholic Church towards all well-intended endeavours to establish reunion on an unsound basis.

The Orthodox Oriental Church does not seek to draw to herself large multitudes who are unprepared to accept the Orthodox truth in its completeness, as the Orthodox Church teaches it, and who would, after such a union had been formed, continue to go their own way, inevitably introducing among Orthodox Christians nothing but uncertainty and confusion. . . . (Nevertheless) the Holy Church does not unlovingly turn away from persons belonging to those other Confessions, *union* with which she regards as impossible. In their case she places no obstacle in the way of their *conversion*.

VIII.

The following short list of recent books and pamphlets will be useful to those who may desire to investigate more fully the grounds of invalidity in Anglican Orders.

'The Question of Anglican Ordinations.' By Canon Estcourt. 1853.
'The Anglican Ministry.' By A. W. Hutton. 1879.
'Reasons for rejecting Anglican Orders.' By the Rev. Sydney F. Smith, S.J. Catholic Truth Society, 1895.
Articles in the *Tablet*, by the Right Rev. Monsignor Moyes, D.D. February 2–May 25, and September 21–December 21, 1895.

(*The above were published before the issue of the Bull* '*Apostolicæ Curæ.*')

'The Pope and the Ordinal.' By the Rev. A. Stapylton Barnes. Robert Browning, 1896.
'A Last Word on Anglican Orders.' By the Rev. S. M. Brandi, S.J. Burns and Oates, 1897.

(*The above were published before the appearance of the Archbishops*' '*Responsio.*')

---

[1] *Op. cit.* p. cli.

Articles in the *Tablet*, by the Right Rev. Monsignor Moyes. February 13–July 17, 1897. These and the previous articles of 1895 will be embodied in a work which is preparing for publication.

'**Tekel.**' By the Rev. Luke Rivington, D.D. Second edition, enlarged and revised. Catholic Truth Society, 1897.

'**Roma e** Canterbury.' By the Rev. S. M. Brandi. **Roma,** 'Civiltà Cattolica,' 1897.

'**No Sacrifice—no Priest.**' By the Rev. A. **Stapylton** Barnes. Catholic Truth Society, 1897.

www.ingramcontent.com/pod-product-compliance
Lightning Source LLC
Chambersburg PA
CBHW020115170426
43199CB00009B/534